# NEW ME

Written and Lived by
DAVID NIROO

Library of Congress Cataloging-in-Publication Data

Names: Niroo, David, author.
Title: New me / by David Niroo.
Description: Ocala, Florida : Atlantic Publishing Group, Inc., [2020] | Includes bibliographical references. | Summary: "This is a spiritual self-help book that evaluates the psychology of people's personalities and how they can change"— Provided by publisher.
Identifiers: LCCN 2020008981 | ISBN 9781620237502 (paperback) | ISBN 9781620237519 (ebook)
Subjects: LCSH: Personality change. | Developmental psychology. | Self-acceptance.
Classification: LCC BF698.2 .N57 2020 | DDC 155.2/5—dc23
LC record available at https://lccn.loc.gov/2020008981

Printed in the United States

PROJECT MANAGER: Kassandra White
INTERIOR LAYOUT AND JACKET DESIGN: Nicole Sturk

*For my wife, Haleh, my sons, Ali and Pasha,
daughter, Azi, and all my soul brothers and sisters.*

# Table of Contents

# Preface

We are here on this Earth as individual human beings. We live for a period of time, one that is full of events, challenges, and our own unique experiences. Our purpose in life is to learn from these events, whether they are good, bad, or ugly. Without these lessons, what are we truly getting out of our journey?

**Life** can be felt as a series of **L**ong, **I**nteresting, **F**rustrating, **E**vents. We need to find our purpose. Our lives, whether short or long, are a journey. On this journey, the key is to stay happy, and we can only do so if we understand ourselves better—learn to deal with our thoughts, emotions, and feelings and learn about ourselves and the world around us. This can be done by understanding how the universe works and asking questions about life: How did we get here? Why were we given the parents we have? Why were we born in the place we were? Why did we grow up the way we did?

At birth you were like a soft dough, full of love and ready to be molded by the world. Day by day, the dough got harder and harder; you adopted a certain belief system based off of your parents, school, society, culture, and religion. This adopted belief system has shaped you into who you are today. At this point, you believe that you are who you are, no longer a soft dough but a hard rock. You need to wake up and realize that inside of you is still the same "loving dough" that was there when you were born. You need to focus on your higher self and make changes for a happier life, a more creative and compassionate life. Learning to love every being and spread your joy, your love, and your happiness with everyone around you.

As long as you do what you've done, you will get what you've got.

My true intention for this book is to illustrate to you that you are a loving person. Living this lifetime on Earth, you came with a purpose; your purpose was to experience certain events that your soul needed to feel, learn, and grow. You are given the freedom to choose to do whatever you desire in this lifetime. However, realize that you are going to experience certain events that your soul desires to complete as a result or consequence of your past actions, your soul's evolution, and your new desires and choices.

We must recognize that all our thoughts and actions have consequences, good or bad; what we say and do to others have consequences. For every action, there must be a reaction. At the younger soul level, you made many choices, and because of karma, you will still experience the results of those choices, whether good or bad. If you do not have darkness, you never see the light. Therefore, nothing in life is bad; it is only experiences, choices, and consequences of our choices. This is karma. So, in this life, you have your past circle to complete (past karma to be cleared), your soul evolution (soul growth level), and consequences of your choices in this lifetime. We learn from all of these as we grow, so at an infant soul level, we go through different experiences and choices than a mature soul level. We will discuss these soul levels in a further chapter of the book. Please note, you may clear some of the past and present consequences, but some may remain for your future lives. To put this into terms that may be more readily understood: If you were in charge of your children and gave them choices to act how they wanted, would it be fair to say they have free will but you make sure they know for every action there would be an equal reaction?

The beauty of life is the ability to make choices. That means we have the ability to experience what we wish, but the main consideration is that these choices have consequences that will come about based on our karma. If you do something loving to someone, you will receive a loving reward or experience, but if you say harsh words or take bad action toward another being, your consequence is to learn how your actions feel on the other side. Once you realize this fact, then you see things differently and try to avoid negative karma going forward. You want to live a life according to the universal law, which we go into detail about later in the book.

## Understanding and Knowledge of How Things Works Makes You Aware in Life

You must look inside to find true happiness. We are often chasing things outside of ourselves that we think will make us happier. Once you find peace inside of yourself, then you will learn to be more observant and less focused on material things and happiness outside of yourself. You will learn how not to suffer from the events in your life, and instead, you will live from the happiness and love that is already in your heart.

You may say that this philosophy is easy to say and impossible to do. Realize there is nothing you can do now to change your events in the past, whether they are good, bad, or ugly. It is done and gone; it's in your rearview mirror. To waste your beautiful energy to rehash and replay the past is nonsense. This concept may be part of your upraising and cultural beliefs, but you can only control your present. So, enjoy NOW and focus on positive future outcomes. This practice will result in positive feelings.

## Whatever Energy We Put Out, The Same Kind Energy Will Surround Us

If we send positive thoughts and feelings out to the universe, then the same type of energy will be attracted to us like a magnet. Every time you find yourself going back to rewind old movies and relive old memories, you waste the valuable present moments of your life. Most people live in the past and daydream about the future; their life in the present gets lost. Every time you find yourself in the past, grab the back of your neck, and bring yourself to the present moment. After a while, it will become a habit to stay tuned in with the present and only focus on NOW.

My dear friend, once you understand the big picture, then it is easy to deal with all the events that have taken place in your lifetime. You will learn how to become happy, content, grateful, and appreciative of the life that you have. This is the "**New You**."

"The Old You" is a wonderful person who has lived as you, until now. You were programmed from childhood to have certain belief systems, taught to feel and react to things in a certain way, and forced by parents, family, society, culture, and schooling to do as you did.

Everything you have done and learned in this lifetime until now is due to the choices you made in this lifetime or experiences that your soul desired and learned from, your karmic experiences and consequences. You will face certain experiences because of past karma and current choices. Things pop up daily because of three things related to your soul: your choice/desire; consequences that are karmic or unfinished; and your soul evolution—the lessons you need to learn to move up. Please, wake up and learn that every-thing in your life is a lesson for you to learn. We came to "Earth school" to have the freedom to do as we wish and learn lessons from our choices, plus our soul evolution lessons.

Here is an example. School, 1st grade through 12th grade, starts in the fall and ends in the spring. During this time, we are to learn different lessons in the school year. In the early years, we learn to write; then as years go by, we get to learn more and more mature subjects and skills. Some of us continue our schooling at a university. During these years, the choices we made from the first grade on were personal choices that have consequences, good or bad. These consequences must be met during this lifetime or a future lifetime.

Earth is a school for us to keep coming back to in order to continue our evolution, experience life, make our choices, and feel and learn the conse-quences of these choices.

It seems as if God separated us from himself and set us free to learn lessons and free us to make as many choices as we wish. What is very important, and what is somehow lost in our life, is that most of us do not understand that things we do or say have consequences, and they all have to be cleared. We are missing the knowledge that all the choices have consequences.

1. We finish our life lessons and schooling (soul evolution).

2. We complete the circle of the consequences of our choices (present and past).

3. We are as pure as the loving person we were when God set us free (the soft, loving dough).

Once we have completed all the above, then we can go back and rejoin him, knowing the fact that God was there in every step of the journey with us, protecting and loving us.

The "New You" means you are aware of this and are grateful for these experiences no matter what. The "New You" has gratitude to everyone that is a part of these experiences. The "New You" has a clear understanding and appreciation for the things that happen and is in total peace with them.

Now it's time to become the "New You" full of peace and harmony.

I am going to keep this transformation as simple as possible, and in the future books, I will go into more detail about all the elements and facts.

The "New You" is going to understand the purpose of this life on Earth, the main reason for the journey is for you to experience certain events that are needed for your soul to feel and experience. Simply said, your soul decided for your physical body in this lifetime to feel certain experiences as a part of your soul evolution on this Earth journey (soul level).

In order to be great at something, you need to learn as much as you can, as this learning leads to understanding. This understanding leads to applied knowledge. In the same manner, your soul wants to learn and understand in order to achieve its greatest potential. Maybe this example can help you understand this concept more practically. Let's say you want to become a good offensive coach in American football. You started your career playing the game yourself, and as a player, you began to learn about every position in the offense.

Over the years, you had the opportunity to play a variety of offensive positions. You chose to be a quarterback, lineman, running back, tight end, or wide receiver. Before each season, you picked your position or positions to focus on. Maybe you even had the opportunity to play in different geographical areas, on different teams, with different coaches, and for good, bad, and mediocre teams. You chose what skills to focus on and learned the types of drills that help hone those skills. You also learned the playbook and constantly reviewed the different types of plays. After years of this, you come to have an incredible understanding of the game. The bottom line, all the choices are open to you when you start, and you use those choices to learn. In the same way, your soul goes through different life cycles to learn to be the best version of itself. As in football, it may take you several seasons (in this case, lifetimes) to learn everything you need to know.

We will learn and realize the power that we have to make choices. This is a power given to us by God; we can make unlimited choices. We will learn not to have attachments to things and people and not to have judgments about things and people. Becoming an observer will help you to be at peace, learning to accept situations as they are and to make better choices going forward.

In the next several chapters, we will learn to understand the universe and our place in it as it pertains to us.

The most important question to be answered is how did we come to these parents, the place that we were born, and the family that we have? Was it the choice of our parents, was it the random selection, or was it all planned ahead?

You have been asking all these questions about yourself, your life, and the universe. Where did your physical body come from? For what reason am I here? Why here or there? Why this family? Personality? Job? Residence? And how is it going to end and why? Perhaps now, you are getting tired of being "normal," and you are searching to find happiness. You may be thinking "if I had this" or "if I had that life would be great." You may be convinced that if you read a book, or listen to a tape, or watch a video, then you can change your life. Until now, none or very little change has occurred from all these attempts. I agree that most of these books and tapes will help you temporarily before you go back to your old self. The main reason for this is a lack of deep understanding of the overall picture and an expectation of outside sources to make the change in your life. As you read this book and understand the basic concept and knowledge of how things work, you will learn how to live your happy, content, and peaceful new life. It is going to be an exciting and loving life.

Once I understood how things evolved around me, why things happened in my life, and how my choices affected my present life and my future, I began to slow down and became more of an observer than a judge. I understood better why everyone acts as they do, accepted things as they were, and made better choices going forward.

Through breathing meditation and alignment of my chakras, I began to release my anger, hostility, and fear, and I started using my biggest source of influence, which is love. From my intuitive intellect, I began having good intentions for my choices and connecting myself to a higher source. In connecting myself with the higher source, I began to manifest my desires and live a life full of joy and love. I still face the consequences and the lessons to learn in my journey, but I am able to digest them better and more calmly.

The biggest change will be a "New You!"

## CHAPTER 1

# My Life

There are two important parts of my life, the experiences I have lived, and the spiritual journey I have gone through and continue to go through. I would like to walk you through both of these, so you can see my path and identify with me.

## MY EXPERIENCES

My life began in Tehran, Iran, on October 13th, 1950. I had a mother, father, and three sisters when I was born. Later, two more sisters came, so it was my father, mother, five sisters, and myself in the family. I was the only son in my family with six children. My father was in the Air Force, and my mother was a stay at home mom. It was not easy for me being the only boy in my family. I felt surrounded by women, which may be the reason I had many different relationships with women in my 20s and 30s.

After having three daughters, my father wanted a son. He was told to go to a mountain that had a temple of Imam Dawood and pray, and he went to this Imam, riding a donkey to the middle of the mountain, praying and asking God for a son. When I arrived on this Earth, he named me Dawood, out of respect for the Imam. In the Persian language, this name is the name "David," so when I came to the United States in 1968, I changed my name to "David," though my family and close friends still call me Dawood.

As a child, I grew up with a family in the upper class. Growing up with my father being an Air Force general, I fell in love with the idea of flying. That's why I wanted to become an astronaut. I wanted to learn to fly as a teenager, but my mother felt it was too dangerous, so I put it on hold. I knew in my heart that one day I wanted to fly.

As a teenager, I was very concentrated on sports. I loved outdoor activities and being active. I was a good athlete. I liked swimming, skiing, and soccer. Not only did I like these activities, but I also was talented in them. I was one of the best swimmers in my club; I went skiing on the weekends at Alborz Mountain, and I played on the soccer team of my high school. When I moved to the United States, I fell in love with American football and tennis. Now, I am close to the age of 70, and I still love to ski and swim.

I went to school at the best high school in Tehran, named Alborz High School. My grades were okay as a teenager. Perhaps this was because I was more focused on having fun than studying. At some point, I decided that in order to come to the USA I needed to improve my grades and studying habits. From my junior year in high school until graduation, I became a straight-A student, which carried on all the way through my college courses.

My dream as a kid was to become an astronaut and study electrical engineering, and at age 17, I was sent alone to Washington, D.C., to start my dream life. After three days of staying with a friend of my father's, I realized it was time to move on. I thanked my father's friend for hosting me, and I took a bus to DuPont Circle in Washington, D.C. I was looking for a room to rent with my broken English and my single suitcase. I found a place with two beds, and I settled into my space. I was resting on one of the beds when a blond man walked in and took a pistol out of his belt strap before setting it on the table. I was shocked. I had just arrived in a new country, and boom, there is a man with a gun in my room. I didn't understand why he had this gun. A few days later, I was riding with him in his car, and I brought my English dictionary with me. I understood from him that he was a private investigator, and that's why he had a gun. It was nice to ride with him in this car. I felt like his assistant. That was a special feeling.

I would only eat at restaurants that had pictures on the wall of what to order because I couldn't speak English very well. Eventually, I improved my English, and I got a job as a busboy. Around this time, I also passed the English exam for foreign students at George Washington University. While I was working at this restaurant, a man used to come every day and sit down to have dinner. One day, he approached me, gave me his business card, and said, "If you want to earn more money, here is my business address." Not wanting to turn down an opportunity, I arrived at his place of work. It was a janitorial company, cleaning office buildings in D.C. They liked my work ethic, so soon I was promoted to assist the floor supervisor. I got a raise, and I moved into a two-bedroom apartment with my private investigator buddy, who had just gotten a divorce. My father paid for my school tuition, but everything else I wanted was on me, and the list of things I wanted started to get bigger and bigger.

I figured out that if I went to school and worked during my free hours in the afternoon as a janitor, I could also get a job as a security guard working 10 p.m. till 6 a.m., all in the same building where I was. At that job, I was able to do my studying between my go around as a guard. This would help me earn the extra money I needed to get the things on my wish list.

The first time I manifested the "law of attraction" was one Sunday afternoon. I was walking around Dupont Circle, and there were a bunch of hippies hanging out—people dancing, playing chess, throwing Frisbees, and walking dogs. Most of the people had long hair and were high on drugs, but this was the place to hang out. As I was walking, I saw the most beautiful car, a white 1964 Chevy Impala convertible with a red interior. I fell in love with it, and I was looking at it closely for at least half an hour while it was parked. The owner eventually came to get in and drive it away. I built up the courage to ask if he would sell the car; he looked at me and said, "You cannot afford this car. It's $1,300."

I replied, "Let me get your number. I may surprise you."

For the next two months, I dreamt about the car day and night; I worked every hour that I could and saved every penny possible. And guess what?

I called the man, and I got my dream car. I did it; I manifested something that I put all my energy into.

Having this car created an extra expense for me, but I worked hard and was able to afford it easily. Driving was fun, especially watching the people look at me in my car. I went to my classes, got good grades, and kept getting promoted at work. Eventually, I was the supervisor for the nighttime janitors, and I only needed to work once a week as a guard, so I had Friday and Saturday night to party and have fun. Life was great. My only worry was that because I drove so fast, the transmission on the car went out and the repairs were expensive.

I decided to sell my car and get a more reasonable one before I headed out to the Midwest. In the summer of 1969, an old friend from my high school in Tehran ran into me in Georgetown. What a surprise! He convinced me to change my college to Oklahoma University, as I would be able to save tons of money and still earn a very good engineering degree. I said, "Okay," packed my stuff up at the end of August, and drove to the Midwest. Driving from D.C. to Norman, Oklahoma was an experience for me. I drove from the mountains and trees of Pennsylvania to Oklahoma with its oil rigs and flatlands. People were nicer; they spoke much slower and had a cute accent. In 1973, I graduated as an electrical engineer with honors. At that time becoming an astronaut was not possible for an immigrant. Meanwhile, I had a cleaning crew working for me, cleaning brand new apartment buildings, and I was making good money. After graduation, I had two interviews with major companies in Texas both offering me $13k a year. Before I accepted one of those jobs, I met a man who wanted to offer me $17k a year to be an electrical engineer for his company. I decided to turn it down because I was making twice that with my cleaning company.

At this point, my degrees became less important to me, and my wish list of things became my priority. I figured that even if I got my master's in electrical engineering, I wouldn't be making much more money, so I decided to get my MBA. I reached out to the old VP of the cleaning company I had worked for in Washington, D.C., and he offered me a position in the carpet cleaning department where we agreed I would take on the advertising and buying new equipment in exchange for my receiving 50 percent of the profit.

And just like that, I was in business and moving towards what I wanted. I was making very good money and getting my MBA at the University of Maryland at night. I had become a big shot at the company due to my success, and I became close friends with the VP. When I was almost through my MBA program, my brother-in-law called me and asked me to arrange 100 trucks for his project in Iran. Accepting the challenge, I talked to two good businessmen in D.C., and we started a company, which would be operated in Tehran by me and in the U.S. with the other two partners. Eventually, I learned how to represent and sell in the world of construction; then I learned how to manage in construction, building condos, roads, and houses on military bases. I continued working in the business field, earning many individual degrees and licenses in different fields. These opportunities, coupled with the strong work ethic I developed with my numerous jobs, blessed me with a comfortable living with a six-figure income.

I have had many good experiences and a few challenging experiences in both my personal and professional life. Professionally, for example, in my first road construction contract, we were to build 22 kilometers of a four-lane highway with other construction companies doing the rest of the 300-kilometer new road. Our 22 kilometers was in the middle of the desert and went through a small town of 300 people who were the last of a group of very bad people that the King of Iran had exiled to that location in 1940. Needless to say, I was among very challenging people, and before us, two other companies had resigned and left. I survived and earned the trust of those around me. It was not easy to work in the desert, drinking water and lemon juice in the heat of the day and shivering through the cold at night. After this great learning experience, my business began as international trade in 1975 when I went back to Iran to set up the company there, and for three years we did it all. You name it, we did it, from making new products to road construction. Then, all of a sudden, in August 1978, I was told by some of my American trade associates that it was best I leave all I had behind and go back to the USA before the revolution took place. So, I moved back to Washington, D.C., in September of 1978. At that time,

I had my two-month old son, two suitcases, and. M, very little money. I sought employment through ads in the paper and found a vague and interesting ad so I decided to respond to it.

The ad said come to meet an executive seeking an individual with a desire to learn his business; what it turned to be, after three vague interviews, was selling door-to-door insurance. They offered me a job, and at that time it was good enough to start feeding my family. I got a job with an insurance company as an agent, hoping to become a good salesman and get promoted to a higher level in management. The product was selling accident policies to individuals for an annual premium of $39, of which I received a $19 commission per policy sold. I was going door-to-door selling this product in the eastern counties of Maryland. I knocked on 50 doors a day, and I was typically able to give 12–15 presentations. Though I sold nothing for the first two weeks, I turned it around and started making 50+ sales per week. Within a year, I became the top salesman, and they made me a manager. After my second year, I became the top manager, then I was made a regional manager in the Northeast. Eventually, four of us became partners, and we were the participating principles for the Northeast region of the company, considered to be one of the top regions. I continued my career in that business until I retired in 2002. I am grateful because to this day, 20 years later, I receive chunks of residual income monthly, and I am grateful to have experienced 20 years of being able to see many agents and managers receive financial rewards beyond their expectations. I thank every one of them for allowing me to be part of their lives.

At age 39, I met my wife, who I am with today. I love her dearly; she is warm-hearted and very loving. Most importantly, she has similar spiritual beliefs as me. I wasn't just fortunate to find someone with similar beliefs, but I found someone who could help me with my own business. In the mid-90s, my wife completed her studies at design school, and I saw her starting to design the most beautiful houses and apartments. Around the year 2000, I felt that new challenges were ahead of me.

As my retirement from the insurance business neared, I began the next chapter of my life. I found myself working a couple of hours a day and having a lot of free time, so I began thinking and dreaming about a new venture that would use more of my time and talent. Meanwhile, my wife was graduating from one of the top design schools, and her first job was a condo in a famous residential hotel. Her project turned into a huge success. She grew up in the south of France and was in tune with classical design. I suggested that she start designing high-end homes, and I would build them.

At that time, I was living in Atlanta, running my Atlanta insurance office. I was walking for two to three hours a day in a big wooden park in the Buckhead area of Atlanta, taking in the silence and allowing the uni-

verse to show me the way for my new venture. We decided to move back to D.C., and she designed our home in Potomac. With my construction background, I built it. It was the talk of the town, and as a result, my construction business started in 2003. For the past 17 years, I have owned my own construction company. With my business and engineering training, I have been building homes, starting from a plot of land and building concrete structures, fences, foundations, and the entire interior of the house. My wife is one of the top designers in the world, and together we build magnificent, classic, high-end homes for our lucky clients. We take pride in our creations, building homes that can stand in pride and beauty for generations to come. Our employees are proud to build and design with us, and we treat them with respect and love. It's a beautiful journey to start a project with the client from scratch and eventually see them so happy in their dream home. As you can see in our website, www.Niroo.net, or www.HalehDesignInc.com, our projects are unique, and the materials being used are the finest from all around the globe. I am very grateful for all the choices I made, as they have brought me to where I am now. These choices have come to me as universal choices, and I have learned from them. (We will discuss a concept called universal living later in the book.)

For the next 20 years, we built the top classical homes in the area. Meanwhile, our lifestyle became more lavish and our income increased. We traveled all over the world seeking the best architectural designs, the best vendors, and the best artists to participate in our unique projects. The satisfaction on being totally involved with a tangible product, seeing a smile of satisfaction on the face of the client who believed they now had a special home was truly satisfying and rewarding. Our clients became part of our family, and we thank them for being part of our life experiences.

Earlier in my life, I wanted to fly, and finally, at age 32, I got my flying license and bought a small plane. For several years, I flew mostly around the east coast of the USA. Through flying, I learned "you can always change your view of things in life." It is so beautiful to be on top of the clouds looking down at the rivers, mountains, hills, and flats. Seeing the beauty of our Earth from the top is surreal and uplifting. Looking up and seeing the beauty of the sky and the stars can force you to appreciate the beauty around you. Flying can also teach you important lessons; for example, no matter the weather, rain, snow, sun, etc., as soon as you get over the clouds, you see the beautiful sky and the shining sun. Flying also taught me how to focus on the positives. You can position your thoughts by focusing below the clouds or looking towards the blue sky and the sun. While doing this, you can remember half a dozen of the most pleasant memories of your life; anytime you feel sad or stressed from unpleasant thoughts, STOP and go to your good memory box and think of those memories and stay there. Think about the clouds, the sky, and the sun. Just as the views change when you are flying, so too can your negative views change to positive views. Speaking of positive views, having to leave Iran so quickly may have been a negative thing for me at the time; however, it gave me the chance to be successful in my new career as an insurance salesman.

Now that I am writing this book, we are in the years 2019 and 2020. My youngest sister lives in the Washington, D.C., area in the USA; two sisters live in Germany; one sister is living in Canada, and one sister has remained living in Tehran. My mother and father had their physical experiences of their life, and they have since returned to the other side to have their summertime in heaven before coming back again in another life. My mother and father were full of love, especially for one another, though my father seems to have been at a higher karmic soul level than my mother.

My father may not reincarnate to the Earth as his soul evolution may have been completed. My mother will continue her soul journey on Earth. My father was a special person and very spiritual, even though he was an Air Force general. In his spiritual journey, he was in a mature life; when I was a child, I saw my father meditate, and sometimes he would be gone for hours. You could not even talk to him during these experiences. He loved and cared for all beings and had a glow around his face. I chose him as a father, and my choice of having him as my father enabled me to experience my life as it is.

## THE DEATH OF MY OLDEST SON:
## ALI SEAN NIROO, AGE 42

On the morning of September 29, 2015, I received a voicemail from my son's wife, Joetta. She said that it was urgent, and I needed to call her. I texted her back, saying that I would call her as soon as I completed my knee therapy.

Ali was born in January 1973 while I was completing my senior year of the engineering school at the University of Oklahoma. I was separated from his mother in 1976, and he and his mother moved back to Oklahoma to a town called Sulphur soon after. I reconnected with my son in 1985, and he would come to stay with me every summertime until he graduated from high school. He was a good athlete, one of the best offensive linemen on the high school level in Oklahoma. He was also getting good grades, but in the last year of high school, he damaged his knee playing football, so he was unable to play football at a college level. He was accepted to Central State University, but in his first year there, he got caught smoking weed.

That was the beginning of his drug journey. He got into a lot of trouble; eventually, he was in and out of jail for drugs. In between his time in jail, he got married, got a divorce, and had a child with his ex-wife. The mother took her son and moved to New Mexico when Ali was sent to jail to serve a long sentence. While he was in jail, he was sending me letters, promising me that he was committed to changing. In 2012, he was released, and I brought him back to the east coast to work for me at my construction company.

When he arrived, he was extremely overweight, weighing over 400 pounds. I wanted him to get a bypass surgery on his stomach to lose weight, and he agreed. The doctor wanted him to lose 30 pounds before he would operate, and that caused him to lose his motivation. Therefore, the surgery process didn't work out because he did not lose the required weight. I guess subconsciously he did not want to do so.

After a few months, I gave him money to go back to Oklahoma and start his own business. I suggested something in marketing, so he didn't have to move his body too much; plus, he was good at selling things. Ali chose to start a landscaping company and moved four times between 2013 and 2015. During that time, he also got married. In 2014, I got a call, and I was told he was in the hospital in Texas. I was also told that he had a heart issue, which was being monitored by the doctors, but in reality, he actually had an overdose. I couldn't get any more information on him and his condition. It was at that time that I began to believe that he had been dishonest during his whole life and had hidden things from me. I was young when I left him, and though I wanted to be part of his life, now I believe I should not have tried to help him as much as I had. I was starting to realize that not much could be done with a grown man. However, maybe I failed, too, on what I could have done. After his overdose, I was sending him my notes about living in harmony and love in an effort to try to support him, but I don't think he was interested.

One day in early September 2015, I got a call from his wife, and she told me that he was in jail again in Oklahoma. She also told me that he may need to go to the ER again because of his heart. The next day she called me and told me he was released from jail because he nearly died of a heart attack. He had been rushed to the ER. The next day, he called me and got angry with me for talking to his wife. He told me that it was his life and that he would do what he wanted. So, I blessed him, and that was the last time I heard his physical voice.

On September 29, 2015, I came out of my knee therapy, and I called his wife. She told me that Ali had died. She started to go into details about how he had died, and I asked her to wait because I was overwhelmed. I told her I would call her back. I did not want to accept the fact that Ali had died. I was crying for many hours. I was crying for everything: my guilt, my love, my pain, all of it. At the time, only my youngest son, who was living in Europe, was in contact with me, but Ali's death brought the whole family together. All three of my kids were together again, and we went to Oklahoma for his funeral. We wanted to celebrate his life as a family. It was a miracle that, in his death, he was able to bring the family together; that was his final gift to me.

This was my speech from his death celebration:

10/03/15

Thank you...

I've learned that a real home is where we came from and where we finally go.

It is full of compassion, joy and love, no jealousy, envy, anger, or judgment, just love.

Ali Sean lived 42 years on the earth. The 42-year old cage was a body for his beautiful soul who wanted to be free and go home. His soul was like a beautiful bird that was stuck in a cage, lost. Now the cage is broken, and he can fly free and open his wing and breath love.

When my father died, I locked myself up in my room for two days and cried. To this day, there is not a day that I do not think and feel him. He was my mentor. When my mom died, I lost my support. I felt like I was hanging from the sky without any support, and now, my son took a big part of my guts out. I can't help it, but I am going to miss him a lot.

I wrote him a letter from my heart and not my mind. It was just a letter to remind him of my true love for him. I am going to burn the letter to ashes and let the spirit of the words in the letter go with him while he is going home.

His purpose was to make sure his family was united at all times. No matter what, he keeps reminding us to be together; he wanted his siblings to show their compassion and love for one another. He kept talking to me about forgiveness. Years ago, if someone did something wrong in my judgment or wrong to me, I would never curse them or harm them. I would only box them out of my sight; that is how I dealt with them. He showed me that I had to forgive others, not because they deserve it, but because I deserve to be in peace.

I love you son, and someday I will join you at home. Meanwhile, I ask my mother and father to welcome you and enjoy you. Thank you for 42 years of being with me on Earth.

Love, Dad

## MY SPIRITUAL JOURNEY

A very important experience for me has been my spiritual learning. In my life, I have always been interested in reading books and expanding my awareness. For the past several years, most of my readings have been focused on understanding myself and the "where's, why's, and what's" of life.

This is how it all began.

Earlier in my life, I felt that the whole world seemingly revolved around me. Somehow, I believed that every aspect of my life was there to support me. The whole world had a role to play for me. Everything I truly desired or wished for manifested itself. I also had a soft spot in my heart for the elderly or people in poverty. As a child, I would sit with the maids and workers of the house and make friends with them. Whenever I met someone that I felt was a good person and they were in need, I would help them with money or give them support. I used to sit down with the elderly members of my family and ask them questions about life. To this day, I always make sure that all of the members of my family are okay. I want to know they are financially secured. I always felt that at a certain point in life people should be able to relax and not worry about how they will get their next meal. I have always believed that young people need to learn to work and earn money, so they can value and appreciate it. These two beliefs are important in my own spiritual journey.

Growing up, religion was a very strong part of my family's daily life. My father was more spiritual than religious. He would study Sufism. He used to meditate, and sometimes he would be meditating for hours. He was so deep into his meditation that when I would watch him it felt as though he was not present. My father was my role model growing up. His personality, honesty, leadership, loving attitude and spirituality became my life standard and level of achievement as a man. Later, I discovered that there is a reason why we chose our mothers and fathers, and we will discuss this later.

When I was 6 years old, we traveled to the Caspian Sea for summer vacation. Suddenly, I came down with a severe stomach virus. I had a very high fever and was rushed back to Tehran to see a doctor. The trip was six hours long, and the travel did not help my illness. By the time the doctors were able to see me, I was in a sort of coma. During this period, I believe I left my body. As I left my body, I could see myself lying down, and I could see everyone else looking at me. I am not sure how long I was gone, but as I floated out of my body, I began to see a tunnel. In the tunnel was a bright beautiful light. As I was traveling through this tunnel, I had a peaceful, loving feeling inside. As I went further down in this tunnel, I started to see my grandparents, who had passed away. They were smiling at me with open arms. I could feel love all over, and I could see images, but I cannot describe them as faces or things I knew. If there is a heaven, as we know it, that is full of love, I was there. I spoke with my grandparents and other bright shining images. Then, I was told to go back. Suddenly, I woke up. I was back at my house, in my bed. It all seemed like a strange dream, yet it felt real at the same time. I did not know what to say or feel about traveling outside of my body. When I told my mother, she told me it was a dream and my grandparents were praying for me in heaven. Somehow, this experience stayed with me every single day of my life. I can still close my eyes and see it happening over and over. I cannot feel what I felt, but I can see it as if I am watching a movie. Sometimes I think that my whole life I have been chasing this love feeling again. Since this experience, I have developed a very strong gut feeling inside of myself. I can feel if something is off or is not right. I am sure one day I will return to this space of love and peace.

I always felt I was special, and that there was a lot for me to learn. I was always curious about other religions and spiritual beliefs. Because of my culture, I was tied to the Muslim religion early in my life. I was taught to have the same beliefs as my parents. I visited the Holy Land of Mecca twice in my life. The first time, I was 31 years old, and I went alone. I did not go through Mecca's entrance ceremony. Instead, I participated in the other important things to do there and stayed for five days. Being there, I felt a strong vortex, a spiritual atmosphere that encouraged me to be in the moment. I was simply being, enjoying the space of worship and the beauty that surrounded me. The second trip was to fulfill my mom's desire to be in Mecca before she died. I gathered all my sisters, my wife, my in-laws, and my son, Pasha, and rented a huge residence suite facing Mecca. My mom was able to fulfill her wish and enjoyed being there with all her loved ones. Both times, the spirituality of Mecca impressed me more than the religious aspects. The most amazing thing is that afterward, I felt lighter as if I had been cleansed from the inside. Simply being in Mecca was the meditation I needed.

In my culture, nobody challenged religion and asked questions. The leaders of the Muslim religion in my country made up rules as they wished, and they connected these rules and laws to the original Muslim religion. The killing and tortures during the late '70s and early '80s brought my country back to ancient times of killing. Many innocent people were killed just because the regime wanted them out of the way. This uncertainty caused many people to flee Iran. Many people just had to drop everything and go; some even changed their religions. In my case, I took my two suitcases and my 2-year-old son and fled the country. I viewed this whole conflict and revolution as an opportunity for people to have a deep look at who they are and what religion they want to be a part of. The situation made me curious about the deeper meaning of this specific religion; I didn't want to focus only on what these leaders were using to influence control. I wanted to really understand religion, so I started to study other religions in order to discover what really resonates with me.

My first step was to understand my family's religion. I began to read the old and new versions of the Koran. I took note of the important points, but generally, I felt the book was more relevant to a much earlier time in humanity. Some rules made sense and were acceptable, and they were also common in other religions. The rules that made sense are a part of the rules or guidelines that make up the Universal Law of Living.

When I came to the USA at age 17, I had the opportunity to meet people with many different religions. I learned and related to Jews, Christians, Buddhists, and Hindus. If you take away all the bells and whistles in these religions, you will find a very similar belief system. This belief system is to be a good person and love and care for others. Religion helps most people to stay in a good direction in their lives. I visited many holy and spiritual places in my life: Mecca twice, temples in Mexico and Thailand, and Sedona a few times, India, Nepal, and Tibet. I've seen the pyramids in Egypt, and I went to Mt. Kailash in western Tibet. All of these beautiful, unique places had their own special high-energy vortex. When I was in these places, my mind would take a break, and I could just feel and appreciate the energy and special history.

In studying other religions and talking to other spiritual leaders, I noticed that most people tend to follow their family's culture and traditions without questioning them. In my personal opinion, going to a church, a temple, a mosque, etc. is a practice more beneficial than harmful, except, of course, in extreme cases where leaders are using religion to brainwash young people to kill or sacrifice themselves in "the name of God."

I also noticed that the fear of going to hell is a driving factor in many religions. As a child, I was told if I did wrong, I would burn in hell's fire. I was told, when I die, I would be evaluated based on a scorecard of good and bad, and if I did worse than good, I would burn and burn for eternity.

This always made me curious about people who unknowingly did bad and ended up in hell.

My next curiosity was about how people were put into their lives. I had many questions about this. For example, why were some people rich or healthy or poor or unhealthy? If we only have one life to live, why were these circumstances given to some and not others? There was no satisfactory answer for my questions—the answer was always "this is how God wants it to be."

My curiosity grew and grew. I did a lot of research, scanning through many religious books, and I was able to find some insight here and there. But deep down, I didn't really understand or find answers. This all changed when I learned about the Self-Realization Fellowship founded by Paramahansa Yogananda. I studied their books for two years, and I learned that God was pure love and the Supreme Intelligence that governs everything. We are like waves, a part of the whole ocean connected to one another. As we hit the shore, we rejoin the main ocean water and form again as another wave. These waves experience different paths and forms each time—symbolic of our spiritual journey on Earth.

I learned about reincarnation. Our bodies are here as a uniform to act and experience life and to learn the lessons needed to bring us to a higher level. When we start a new life, we go into a new body to learn new lessons and have new experiences.

Then, I learned how to meditate and look inside myself. In meditation, I learned that breathing is the source of my energy. I spent my life breathing fast and shallow. I was always in a rush. I started to breathe more deeply and slowly, becoming aware of my breathing. This brought more oxygen to my cells, improved my energy, and helped me get fit.

Finally, I was introduced to love as a driving force, rather than hate and revenge. The most important part of this was learning that every being has a soul and our souls all belong to one greater spirit. We are all in a web of love, experiencing what our soul was set to gain. What connects us all is love. Love is the common factor in all beings.

Our being is like a castle with three gates: the gate of the body, the gate of the soul, and the gate of the mind. We need to access our life force in order to keep our body's battery charged. Deep sleep, sunlight, oxygen, water, and food are subsidiary sources of energy. The most important source is deep sleep, as this is where we get most of our cosmic energy. Next is proper deep breathing, which gives our cells energy to function. Water, sunlight, and organic food are the most helpful in keeping our bodies healthy.

I do my meditation, live my life at the present time, act as an observer rather than judge, have a love for all beings living life. I am "being fair and firm according to the Universal Law of Living." Meditation helps me to be in the moment, feel the joy, and love life. I find happiness inside of myself. It's not outside of me.

People have said that if you repeat a task every day for 90 days it will become a habit, so I tried very hard every second, for months to stay in the present time, think of only good things, and focus on my desires to manifest. Before I knew it, it became my habit of mind only to focus on the present, find positive solutions, and stay on the path for my desires to be manifested for my highest good.

## CHAPTER 2

# I Have the Power;
# You Have the Power

Understanding my life became my mission. I needed to know how I was created and why. Who and what makes "me" as a being? Is it my body, mind, soul, or all above?

Now, while you're reading this book, I urge you to put your judgments aside. Keep your mind open. That's the key to the "New Me."

## UNDERSTANDING THE MIND'S POWER

In my studies of the mind, I learned that the mind is divided into three parts: consciousness, subconsciousness, and superconsciousness. In order to better perform daily duties and acts of life, we should have good memory, which is recalling the experiences from the conscious, subconscious, and superconscious.

Consciousness is in the nerves, muscles, and senses during wakefulness. It is thinking and reasoning while we are awake and aware of what we are doing. When we are using the conscious mind, the ego (ego has many names: my body, my name, my nationality, etc.) orders certain activities through the senses, which are carried out through the thought and muscle processes.

Subconscious is the vault of the past and present memories of all our experiences. The subconscious is always awake, both in the daytime as a memory vault and at night as dreams or as a feeling of peace when you're deeply sleeping.

Your superconscious is always guiding you toward your highest good, watching the conscious and subconscious minds. It is calm, peaceful, and highly intuitive. Its source is located on the point between the two eyebrows, sometimes referred to as the "third eye." The soul manifests super consciousness through its intuitive process. Superconsciousness and intuitions are therefore one in the same.

We must keep all these minds open to be creative, intuitive, and blessed.

## UNDERSTANDING THE POWER OF YOU

The more I studied the more I was amazed by how interesting this life is. I learned not to poison peace by being angry. I stayed quiet when I was angry, and I chose to stay away from people who always complained about life and were never grateful. Remember, whatever you want others to be, first be that yourself. The power is within each of us; we control how we feel, and we control our perception of the world and our circumstance. We also control our own karma by the decisions we make daily.

This all may seem very abstract to many of you. But believe me, there is a reason that you are on this earth. We must all learn our lessons. Our gift from God is to be filled with love. That's the way of God. We have to go through our ups and downs of course in life, but these events make us learn. And it's important to learn.

One of my biggest lessons was learning to accept things as they are. What is, is. That's it. If you accept this, you will be able to learn from difficult situations in life; instead of fighting them, you will accept them and be able to move on. Remember, you can only really change how you perceive a situation. The glass is either half full or half empty; it's your perception.

How you deal with each situation is your choice, your responsibility. I am not saying ignore the part where you feel the glass is half empty or ignore the part where you feel the glass is half full. Accept both, stay calm, be open-minded, observe more, and move on. Make choices that will help you to move forward with a positive intention and focus, and this will be your driving force in learning and growing in your life.

When you're done reading this book, you will feel more connected to your heart and intuition. You will be able to accept life as it comes and get more clarity on what there is for you to learn from these experiences. You will also have more knowledge about cosmic energy and how to have clean good energy in your body and your environment.

Remember, whatever you want others to be, first be that yourself. More importantly, whatever you want to be, you have the power to be.

## UNDERSTANDING THE POWER OF MEDITATION

Being open-minded is important. Changing yourself takes courage. You have to have the courage to look inside and find out why certain things affect you. Why do you have certain habits? Where do they come from? How do you live your life in ways that don't allow you to learn and be happier and loving? Once we understand ourselves better, we can focus our energy on what makes us feel happy and balanced.

As mentioned before, from ages 28–51, I was in the insurance business. Part of my job was to motivate people to be more self-confident in presenting themselves and their products. I have studied many motivational books, and I can say I was a good motivator myself. What I found was that most people eventually went back to their old habits, even though they changed for a short time. It was as if they were just patching over the parts of them that they did not like. To create the New You, we need to dig deep into your heart and take all the good that you are, so you can feel and appreciate how special you really are.

Now, I wasn't asking these people to do anything I hadn't done myself. It was very challenging to deal with the power of my old habits. I had developed them early in life, and they were a result of my family, friends, and companions, as well as my soul. To break these habits, as well as understand them, I turned to meditation, which has remained an important part of my life. Meditation helped me a lot.

There is an old belief that God will give you what you ask for. But how does that work?

Today we are learning that everything is made of energy. When you think of something, that thought is energy. This energy starts to go into creation based on your thoughts and beliefs. For example, if you want something and you have contrasting thoughts like, "I want this to happen" and "what I want cannot happen because...", you are sending mixed messages into the universe. Your energy will go in two directions and cancel each other out.

It's important to first find out what you really desire. Is it based on good intentions? Is it based on the Universal Law? Could it help others besides you? From there, you can start visualizing and focusing on this desire. Be very aware of your mind and how you value yourself. It takes a lot of energy to focus in one positive direction, but if the desire is for your higher good and comes from your heart, it will be much more likely to become a reality, and your desire will be manifested. This is where meditation becomes a powerful tool.

In order to really change your reality, you have to address your deeper beliefs. Motivational work and speaking usually only make a short-term difference in someone's life because it only addresses the conscious mind. So, for a time, you are able to change your behavior, but eventually, you slip back into old patterns that relate to your deeper beliefs. These belief systems live in your subconscious mind, not in your conscious mind. Someone once said to me, "You become exactly the person of the real picture you carry of yourself inside of your heart." I did not truly understand then, but I do now. What he meant was that my true self resides in my subconscious mind.

Visualization through meditation is a great way to start to change your subconscious beliefs, to actually see yourself living your goal or your wish and to feel it in your heart and in your body. For example, if you want to sell your house, sit down in the evening to relax your body and start to think of happy thoughts, things that make you smile. Once you have reached that space and your body and mind are relaxed, start to visualize yourself selling the house, moving out, receiving the check, smiling at your partner, thanking the house for the period you and your family lived in it, blessing it to the new owner's with love. Feel and see all of it. What this does is it brings these images to the frontal lobe of your mind, and you begin to press them into your subconscious. So slowly, slowly you start to actually believe you are in the process of selling your house.

Now, another part of this process is understanding that in your heart you are a good person. If what you're visualizing isn't good for you and the world around you, you won't be able to manifest this goal. Your heart and subconscious mind will not really take it in and create the energy flow you need. Because somewhere your wishes go against who you really are, a good loving soul. Don't let your doubting conscious mind sabotage you. Don't let others' judgments of you hold you back. You are a unique person, and you have the right to get what you want and need in your life.

We often ask ourselves how sometimes, even with good intentions and a positive focus, we didn't get what we want. When you want something, you have to let the fear and anxiety of not getting it to go. In order to do that, imagine the worst possible outcome of you not getting what you want. Imagine it; feel it. Finally, accept this outcome and let it go. You have to be ready to accept anything and learn from it without judgment or resentment. Once this is done, your subconscious fear energy will be lower, and it won't affect the results as strongly as before.

Here are some steps to complete this process:

1.) Sit down, be still, and think of something that makes you smile or be happy.

2.) Create a good intention that is not only good for you but is good for everyone and everything involved in the situation.

3.) Visualize yourself not getting what you want, feel it, and consciously let the fear go and accept what is.

4.) Focus on what you want. Feel it and welcome it.

5.) Visualize yourself getting everything you want related to the situation; see yourself enjoying it and manifesting it.

You will most likely get what you put your intention and focus on. If the outcome does not work out, as you desire, then accept that too. God knows better; the universe knows better. Accept that this was a learning opportunity and understand that, in the long run, it's better for you this way.

We are here to learn lessons—remember that; that's the real goal. You cannot appreciate the light unless you have seen the darkness. Imagine all of your uninhibited energy flowing in one direction; you have the power to do that. The universe will manifest what you want and need in a way that is best for you and everybody else. Look at all this power you have by meditating and understanding your own power. I know certain challenges get us bent out of shape, and we get overwhelmed. But wouldn't it be better to keep the boat steady during the storm? We can learn how to approach situations in a much calmer state of mind, with better focus and less fear. We can learn to feel good regardless of the outcome. "New Me" will be able to stay calm, meditate, and become an observer rather than being engaged and judgmental.

Meditation does not just help us achieve our potential; it can also allow us to connect to others. In meditation, I could focus on the fact that behind the mask of everyone is the soul of a brother or sister. In the spiritual world, all that is between our souls is love, so by using this tool to focus on others I can fill my mind—conscious, subconscious, and super subconscious—with love. During this practice, I remember that in this lifetime individuals are going through the experiences set for them, and if we understand this, then we will not judge and, instead, will send our love and blessing to them.

## UNDERSTANDING THE POWER OF LEARNING

My life has been full of challenges. Maybe you think it's easy for me to write all of these things and believe in them because I am doing well in my life, but the truth is that I had many periods in my life where I felt very challenged.

Imagine how you would feel living in a country where you don't understand the language, and you use your last $100 to find a job in Chicago during college Spring Break. Imagine not having enough money to eat and imagine not being able to talk to the person serving you food. Imagine staying in a room with four guys and buying hot dogs, which you had to put on top of a water heater in the room to warm them up in order to eat. Imagine leaving it all to go back to Oklahoma to go to college. Imagine going back to your home country and spending three years building a great business, only to be told there is going to be a revolution. Imagine packing a few bags and leaving with your family for their safety, leaving all you built behind and starting all over from nothing back in the USA. Imagine knowing you could not get anything back from what was behind.

This wasn't the only challenge in my life, and maybe I should change the word "challenge" to "learning opportunity." I had a strained relationship with one of my sons for over 30 years; it finally came to a boiling point. He wanted to be free of fatherly control, and he broke the relationship. We did not speak for about five years, and I missed the birth of his first child and his wedding. I missed him, and sometimes the situation would make me cry. I would ask God to put more love in his heart.

Eventually, we reconciled because of my oldest son's troubled life, which I shared earlier.

At this time, I was also transforming into the "New Me," and my son's heart was opening to love. The sudden death of my oldest son reunited all of us. It's sad that his death was the major cause of this reunion, but that was also his gift to our family. He created peace, and we all could feel the love for each other underneath the anger that past experiences had created.

At the time all of these events were very challenging for me, sometimes even devastating. When I look back at them now, I wish I knew back then what I know now. I would have handled each situation with more grace and a calmer attitude. I would have been more relaxed and focused, and I could have enjoyed the ride. In some cases, I would have made different decisions and changed the outcome. I learned that I don't have to win each battle in life; it's more important to win the war and have fun doing it.

As I share with you my own journey in this life, you may see some similarities. You may be able to understand why it was so important for me to search and find truth. I wanted to know why I am living, why I feel the way I feel, what will really make me happy in life. I needed to start to take away the old lens I had over my eyes and look at my old belief systems. I had to let them go. I needed a new lens to feel better and understand what is really happening. Now, I can see the world and myself much better.

It's easier said than done. But in the end, we have nothing to lose and only gain knowledge and understanding through learning. What you can gain is so important, and that's what counts. If you wouldn't be interested in this, then you wouldn't be reading this book. I truly believed that you are so blessed, as am I. We are fortunate to be able to share these ideas, learn to shine as we really are, and help others as well.

If you speak with most successful people, they will tell you that their greatest lessons came from times of failure. They kept going; they did not give up. When you lose today, it's just a stepping stone for you to go forward tomorrow. If you fail, get angry or afraid, and don't try again and again, you won't ever get to reach your potential; you won't find the glory of what the universe has in store for you. We can learn to combat this little voice in our heads telling us "no, don't do it; you will get hurt, stay back."

What if I told you a secret? There is a waiting list for souls to come to this earthly life and experience what you and I are experiencing. You are probably saying, "Wow! How is that possible?"

We will explore this subject later on in this book, but I just wanted to give you a little shot to wake you up, so you can appreciate what you have and what you have gone through in your life, regardless of how your life looks in this present moment.

Think about it. We all come to this Earth naked and leave it the same way. What we bring at birth is our soul, mind, and body, and in the end, we take our soul and our mind (the subconscious, the library of our lives) and leave the body to become dust. The body is the vehicle for our earthly life. We need to keep it healthy and strong, so we can experience more events, and our soul can experience its evolution. We must also complete the circle (our past karma), and the more we learn the better chance we have to advance our soul.

I believe that I am passing on a message that should be passed on to others. We are all connected; our souls are connected because we all came here to give a gift to others and the world. Just like you and I have the responsibility to be happy, we also have a responsibility to share this happiness with others, to share what we have learned.

Life is enjoying our experiences and having whatever we wish to have. However, our negative energy and belief systems can create a reality that we don't want. Most people think money is the main thing that would make them happier in life, but trust me, with all the money and fame that I had while I was separated from my son, I had a horrible cloud over my head, a big knot in my stomach, and an ache in my heart. Money and fame could not make me truly happy. God's light shining on me and opening my son's heart was the only thing that could give me real peace. So, you cannot buy happiness; happiness is finding true inner peace within yourself and being grateful for what the universe presents to you in each moment.

We are all searching for happiness, but most of us don't even know what real happiness is. We think we know what it is, and once we believe that, once we have it then we can relax. But what I have learned is that happiness is not something we can get from the outside– it starts by being happy on the inside and enjoying the outside challenges as they appear in our life. Happiness is a moment-to-moment experience. Some experiences make us joyful, and some experiences bring our energy down and can make us disappointed, but that's life. The key is to appreciate all of it, the good and bad, and focus on being grateful for what we have been given and what we have gone through. Our attachments and expectations create unhappiness, so we need to learn to accept what life gives us without getting hurt or disappointed. We need to learn to become an observer of events, observing the entire picture, and taking moments to stop and pause. We must look at things from a higher point of view instead of getting lost in a reaction. When we learn to pause and be an observer, we can see each situation with-out judgment and make decisions based on our intuition or inner faith. Observing gives us the luxury to step out of our old self and our old belief systems, so we can take action and go forward in the best way possible. For so many years we have learned from society, parents, religion, and other influences to judge everything as either good or bad, so most people spend all their time judging and reacting to situations. I won't lie, it's hard to step out of this mentality and way of thinking, but that's why it's so important to create a "New You." Becoming this person is the answer.

Most people are not focusing on the present moment and what they are doing here and now. People are usually daydreaming, and unfortunately many are thinking about negative things, situations that are from their past, or things they have anxiety about doing or saying. These days, day-dreams bring our energy lower. This changes if you focus on what you are doing. Stay present, but when you drift off, do it consciously and focus on what you want, what would make you the happiest.

A happy life is a chain of happy moments and happy experiences.

1.) **MAHATMA GANDHI:** *"Happiness is when you think, what you say, and what you do."*

2.) **MICHAEL FOX:** *"My happiness grows in direct proportion to my acceptance, and in inverse proportion to my expectations."*

3.) **ABRAHAM LINCOLN:** *"Most folks are as happy as they make their minds up to be."*

4.) **CARL SANDBURG:** *"The secret of happiness is to admire without desiring."*

5.) **MARGARET YOUNG***: "Often people attempt to live their lives backwards, they try to have more things, or more money, in order to do more of what they want, so they will be happier."*

6.) **DENIS WAITLEY:** *"Happiness cannot be traveled to, owned, earned, worn, or consumed. Happiness is the spiritual experience of living every minute with love, grace, and gratitude."*

7.) **FREDERICK KEONIG:** *"We tend to forget that happiness doesn't come as a result of getting something we don't have, but rather of recognizing and appreciating what we have."*

8.) **LUCIUS ANNAEUS SENECA:** *"True happiness is to enjoy the present, without anxious dependence on the future."*

9.) **THICH NHAT HANH:** *"There is no way to happiness, happiness is the way."*

10.) **MANDY HALE:** *"Happiness is letting go of what you think your life is supposed to look like and celebrating it for everything that it is."*

We see happiness through our own lenses. For the New Me, I have defined happiness as something you cannot wear, buy, travel, or own; happiness is to feel love and gratitude at the present moment on the inside, no matter what is happening outside of you, because you are only an observer for outside elements and are not attached to them.

I appreciate my life, and I thank God for the opportunity to experience life with all its challenges.

I was going through life in the fast lane; using my "law of attraction." I was quickly crossing things off my wish list like learning to be a pilot and buying a plane. I was flying through life, and life was great financially. I noticed something about my personality—I had an eagle's eye. An eagle has the best-magnified eye, it can see the smallest prey from a mile high, and once he spots it, he focuses and dives 100 percent full speed towards it. That's how I was with everything that I desired to have. I had the ability to spot something that I wanted, focus on it, and dive with all my energy and focus to get it. Without good intention and focus, I would not have been able to accomplish what I did in my life. I was one of the top salesmen. I read and listened to many great motivational books and audio discs to learn and become a better person than I was. However, the health aspect of my life was not great.

I was smoking three packs of cigarettes a day, and I drank alcohol as much as I could, whenever I could. Meanwhile, I was going through divorces, one after another, until 1990, when I married my lovely wife, whom I have been with for the last 30 years. She has a heart of gold, and she is very knowledgeable in nutrition and well-being and is one of the best international interior designers. I am grateful to have her as my partner in life. She supported me in my passions and put up with old me until I transformed into the New Me. I thank her for her patience and love.

By the way, I quit smoking cigarettes in 1993; I quit cold turkey, no longer smoking three packs a day, before my youngest son was born. I also quit drinking cold turkey in 2003, and I have not taken another sip of any kind of alcohol since then. I guess I can say I have some Forrest Gump in me; once I decide to do something, I do it totally, and once I'm done, "I am done."

Since 2004, I began reading more and more books about life, happiness, religion, and spirituality. I started to wonder how I could get as close as possible to a constant feeling of being happy inside. I wanted to feel in peace and harmony, at ease and content. I wanted to be fulfilled in the moment. When I look back at my life, it has been similar to most of you. Chasing more money, more vacations, more of this, more of that. I found myself thinking nonstop, and 95 percent of my thoughts were the same thoughts over and over again. I was always trying to figure out what was next. One day, I remember seeing a beautiful tree right by the driveway, so I asked my wife when she planted the tree. She said, "It's been here for three years." I was surprised. I must have passed by this tree hundreds of times driving out of our long driveway, and I never noticed because I was always busy with what was next.

Even when we took a vacation, we would check into hotels, and immediately I would try to set up what we should do next, where to eat, where to shop, where to go. My wife kept having to remind me, "we are on vacation—relax." Eventually, I learned this from her, and now I understand that the purpose of a vacation is actually to relax. There is nothing wrong with going to a nice place and planning where to go, but relaxing is the whole point, enjoying the moment. I think most of us don't really know how to relax and enjoy the moment. We do not really know how to enjoy a vacation.

In essence, I did not know how to control or slow down my mind. I couldn't give it a rest. Even when I was lying on the beach, I would have loud music in my ears or I would read a book. Very rarely would I be able to just lie down, feel the wind, enjoy the sun, and watch the beautiful waves coming and disappearing again. The power of waves and the sound of the ocean is one of the best relaxation tools, but we are too busy and miss it. I would walk along the shores and watch others being busy in their minds, probably planning the next day or next thing to do. We are programmed to think of what is next; we do not know how to stop our minds and feel the present. Meditation teaches you how to do this; you learn to stop your mind and feel the present.

The truth is, the more successful you become, the more responsibilities you have and the more you carry in your mind. That's why the biggest task is to realize the balance in life. Life offers harmony to us. Harmony in our mind, body, career, and life. The truth is, I never really understood that until recently.

I realize life has a much faster pace in the USA compared to Europe. People in Europe take a long, relaxing break for lunch, and they enjoy dinner with friends and family. These dinners can be hours long, not just a quick bite to eat. Life for them is to enjoy; they work, so they can enjoy life. Entertainment, food, and vacation are all important for them, and most Europeans take the entire month of August off for vacation. If you ask Europeans, what is the most important time of the year, most of them will say August because that is when they can relax and enjoy life, not think about work. In the United States most of us "live to work." Usually, we eat lunch while we work and have a short dinner, so we can finish up some more work. We live like this day after day; we are part of the rat race, without even knowing that there is another way. My wife says that we need to take our time while having dinner with the family, time to appreciate and be grateful to the universe for the family and food. She believes we need to stay present, bless the food, and all that contributed to having our food, chew, and enjoy every bite to the fullest, focus, and appreciate the moment. This will help our well-being and digestion. We should not indulge and think of what is next; we should enter good thoughts and feel the love at all times. We have a choice that God has given us to choose our thoughts and actions. If we choose to stay present, think of all the good things we desire, and feel inside the love and gratitude for all we have, we are choosing to become new. That is how you become the New You.

I remember growing up, we would watch TV for maybe an hour, usually a good TV show or a soccer game. In the '60s through '80s, TV started to take more of people's free time. People started cutting family time and turning it into TV time, and back then there were only landline telephones, so if you were not home or at the office, the machine would take a message. Back then, the main distraction from being together and enjoying the moment was the TV.

In the 2000s, the internet and cell phones came and changed the entire world once and for all. They both changed the family culture, society, and the exchange of information. I have no problem with new technology and the internet world—it puts the information you want in the palm of your hands. But I do realize that life is to be experienced, and the internet world is taking over our free time. We constantly look at our smartphones, looking at them on the bus, train, plane, in restaurants, and at dinners and weddings. We are busy all the time texting, posting on Twitter, or scrolling through Facebook, and we miss the most important part of life, being here and now.

When was the last time you stopped and looked around? When was the last time you asked yourself, "Who is the architect of this universe? Who could have so much knowledge to create the ways the trees live and how they get new leaves in spring to lose them in fall? How do they go through the seasons just by the energy that is provided by nature? What about how water evaporates from the ocean creating clouds or how the wind moves the clouds over the Earth and the clouds produce rain that nurtures the plants and the land? How are there so many beautiful birds? Why can't artists fully capture the beauty of the colors on these birds or in nature?" We need to take more space to enjoy the wonders of life and nature. Just imagine the sea colors: blue, green, clear, and gray. At shores all around the world, the beautiful colors play on the beaches. Trees are vibrant green in spring, and the most beautiful colors of red, orange, and yellow coat the trees before the leaves in fall in autumn. No man could ever design or create such beauty. The universe has given us this beautiful Earth with all its wonder, and some of us trash it or ignore it instead of appreciating it, loving it, and take good care of it. This is our *home*. It belongs to every one of us, and it is our job to feel that way and make sure it remains safe and beautiful for generations to come.

I have had the pleasure of building high-end homes; my wife and I have traveled all around the world with her seeing the most beautiful homes, palaces, interior and exterior designs, and architecture. I have seen countless designs around the world, but if I stacked all these amazing designers, builders, and architects on top of each other, they would not even come close to creating the magnificence of the design of the beautiful nature on Earth. It seems as if God has hired the best to create this beautiful nature:

the colors, smells, mountains, flowers, oceans, lakes, all animals, and all beings. Each is a different color and shape for just us to observe. We can even use nature; there are natural organic medicines to heal us.

I am getting goosebumps talking about how genius and capable God is to be able to manifest this universe. The physical world that we see with perfection and the science that was used to create it is amazing. To this day, we are finding new things out, new scientific facts about this Earth. We are discovering that everything in fact has a consciousness. The more we slow down and look at what is already around us, the closer we get to the creation of it all.

In my life, I was so busy achieving my higher goals that I totally consumed myself with the rat race of life and my business. My attitude was "if I don't get ahead, then maybe I miss something or someone else gets ahead." Unfortunately, I was racing against everybody else, and there was no time to slow down. I became like a kid in a candy store, buying things, and wanting to travel. But when I was alone, I could feel a knot in my stomach, mixed emotions. Somehow, I felt a sense of guilt and anxiety; there was also an emptiness there. The more I gained, the more there were challenges and problems to solve. I was running out of time to catch up with it all. Something was still missing. I was going from goal to goal, and once got what I wanted, I was satisfied only for a short time, then it was on to the next one. My desires became the focal point of my life. I would usually pick very challenging goals, and I ended up with a lot of anxiety and turmoil about it. Many nights were difficult with headaches and worry. And on the rare occasion that I didn't get what I wanted, I would feel horrible about it, devastated both mentally and physically. I became addicted to chasing things, and in tough times, the only thing I knew how to do is to be tough. I was told as a kid "don't show weakness; don't think of the past. Yesterday is a canceled check, and tomorrow is a promissory note. Keep going. Have a good attitude; show no weakness, and fake it until you make it." This, I realize now, is the wrong mentality.

Being a successful marketing manager, I read many motivational books and was able to give good daily and weekly sales seminars, trying to boost morale and motivate the sales force to go out and be more enthusiastic. I invited them to put their problems in a box and only focus on one sale at a time. I told them, "the more no's you get, the closer you are to a yes." It's the law of averages, so for x amount of no's you will get, y amount of yes's. I told them to take one day at a time and leave their personal problems in the car.

Well, that all works great, but what happens when you get back in the car, pick them up, and go home to your family? How do you deal with it? Do you take your frustration out on them, shove your problems under the carpet and act like everything is fine? Or do you drink to numb yourself out? Bottom line, if we are afraid to deal with our problems, they will bottle up and add up. There are successful people who truly cannot get things done in 24 hours, so their time and mind are all about work. They have no time to rest and meditate, no time for the family, and no time for themselves.

You learn how to deal with "problems" no matter what your status is. But what we do is we keep pushing ourselves going for what we want while underneath it all our issues keep popping up. They may be unresolved issues from our past, our hidden emotions, or shameful and painful memories.

So, what did I do? While I was motivating all of these salesmen, I practiced what I preached. I went out, did my work, and came home. I numbed everything out with a couple of glasses of alcohol and went to bed, then I did it all over again the next day, and the next day, and the next day. I would wake up in the morning, look in the mirror, and say to myself "to be enthusiastic you must act enthusiastic! Oh boy, am I enthusiastic!" I would repeat it until I could feel it. But this can be exhausting, and in 2003, I made a decision, no more "fake it till you make it." I didn't want to have two lives and live the way I was. So, I stopped drinking, and I decided to be honest with myself. Then I started to look at what I really wanted in my life and what was important for me. I had to make a decision to live my life and face myself. I realized suppressing my issues for financial success was not healthy—mentally, physically, or spiritually.

In life there are four important pillars that must be balanced in order for you to be complete; financial success cannot be the only pillar that you pay attention to. These four pillars that hold you up and must be balanced are: health, spiritual welfare, finances, and family. You must make sure you pay attention to all of them and balance them in your life. You cannot pay attention to one or two and ignore the rest, or your life will not be balanced.

After deciding this, I realized that I have control over all my choices.

So, I started to play a mental game with myself. If I had one year to live, how would I live it?

I realized that in order to be my best self, I had to accept who I am. If I had one year to live, I didn't want to be busy with the past and blaming others. I want to love people, love myself, and respect myself. I realized I've done bad things, good things, ugly things, but I have to accept who I am and decide to live, taking total responsibility for my life. I decided not to be a victim anymore and go for what is good for me and everyone else. I am who I am, with all my flaws and good qualities, and there is nothing I can do to change the past.

I knew one thing for a fact, I loved God, and God had always been there for me. I just needed to trust him and actually trust myself that I could do it. I thought that if I make good choices from here on out and if I decided to make choices with my focus on positivity, I could make it. I would ask myself before I did something, "What would David, who loves himself, do in this situation?" Then I thought, if I can do this for a year, it will become a habit for me. And it worked; it's in my system now.

So, if you had a year to live, how would you live it? I'm sure you would make different choices than you would have before, and you would appreciate the moment more.

There is nothing wrong with making money and desiring to have things. It's nice to live comfortably, be able to afford nice things, and be able to go on various vacations. But chasing for more and more, that's the part that can change. Starting to live your life in the moment with positive vibrations will make you happier, and the desires you have can be supported with visualization and meditation.

I also acknowledge that the process is not like a switch that we can just flip on or off. It takes time to change. I needed to take my time to learn about myself again. I needed to learn about the emotions that are inside of me, and what I really want in my life. I needed to learn how to stay calm in stressful situations and focus on what is important. I needed to learn how to enjoy the beauty in what I see and feel.

A wise man wanted to teach his children a big lesson about life and the way they should approach things they desire. On a sunny bright day, he asked all of his children to come to the backyard; they had a good-sized grass backyard. He laid down a blank white piece of paper about 10 feet in front of them. Then he asked them to burn the paper without getting any closer to it. It was clear there was nothing they could do, so their father took a magnifying glass and used the power of the sun to burn the paper. His children were amazed. The father explained that the sun shines all the time; the same energy is shining everywhere, and if you take this energy and focus, like a magnifying glass, on one thing it can do miracles. He used the focus of the magnifying glass to burn the paper. He taught them how to use their energy on what they desire, so it would be manifested.

When you're traveling, see the scenery, enjoy the trip; when you are with family or friends, focus only on them, the most important person in the world is the one you are within the given moment. And do the same at work, at sporting events, and when making love. When you think about it, there is nothing else you can do except for what you are doing, so why occupy yourself with something else?

## CHAPTER 3

# Who Am I?

Most motivational books and findings have similar concepts. Each having a different twist to them, but the main message is more or less the same. Many take specific aspects, make them the focal point, and expand upon them.

I spent the last 15 years reading many of these books, and I could see that the more I read, the more deeply I could understand what was actually being said and taught. I read and studied over 375 books. One of my main searches was to look for the ultimate energy source and our relationship to it. I call this source "God," though people may have another name for it. Looking back at my near-death experience when I was a kid, I related that experience to what I was reading in the books. I learned that there was something more to life and this world than I knew at the time. Sometimes when I travel to different cities or countries, I get the feeling that I have been there before. Many books tell of people with similar stories, and I've come to realize that I have had past lives, and I was in these places during my past lives. These memories lie in my subconscious.

Sometimes when I dream, it feels so real. Sometimes I see my dead parents and they talk to me; they tell me exactly what I need to hear at that time. Sometimes it doesn't make sense at all. Could it be that my astral body or my soul was traveling while I was dreaming? If it is or isn't, how can I know? I had to move away from a certain kind of religious belief that I was raised around and find out with an open mind what is real and what is not.

Now, I remember being told the same as many people were told, that my religion was the best. If I ever questioned this belief, then by rules of the religion I would be a sinner. This may eventually cause me to burn in hell. So, even though they told me that God was great and had mercy, that God was kind and would forgive my sins, on the other hand, they said God was a harsh ruler who would send me to hell to burn for my wrong choices. This fear of punishment was instilled in me, and I believe this fear of punishment is in all of us, deeply causing each of us a sense of fear or anxiety.

What helped me break free of this fear is a beautiful story.

A religious old man had a son, who was a bit of a disappointment. This was because the son would come home drunk every night. One day the man said to his son, "Look, what you're doing is sin, and if you continue, God will burn you in hell."

His son seemed not to care and continued doing the same thing every night. One day the old man was sitting on his front porch, and suddenly, two men came by to say hello and started a conversation. The old man shared with the two travelers that he was very concerned about his son, that his son was drunk all the time, and that he feared God would punish him with eternal hellfire. He shared how scared he was that his son was doing so many wrong things while he was drunk, and he believed that with every sin his son would burn more and more. So, one of the travelers asked the old man if he had an oven.

The old man replied, "Yes."

Then the traveler asked, "Can you heat it up? Is it a big oven?"

The old man said, "Yes, it's a big oven, and I can heat it up very hot."

So they asked the old man to heat up his oven, and they waited with the old man all night. Eventually, his son arrived, and the two men grabbed his drunk son and started to bring him towards the hot oven. When the old man realized they wanted to put him in the oven, he screamed and cried and said, "No, please don't do this." Then they dropped his son, and one of the wise men smiled and said, "God loves all his children way more than we do as parents. If we cannot see our kids burn alive, how could God ever witness or do that." The old man was shocked, and with tears in his eyes, he realized what the travelers were saying was true.

When I heard this story, it dawned on me; this belief of punishment was just a belief. I do not deserve to be punished, and I can let go of this belief and all the anxiety I carry around it. God loves me, and God loves you. We are here to learn from our mistakes, not to be punished for them. Our guilt and our shame are the real fire. We are burning ourselves already. Remember, God knows only one thing, unconditional love.

Another big question I had about life was "Why are people as they are?" Why are some healthy, some not healthy, some financially well off, and some not as fortunate?" For example, a very nice person could be poor, and a very crude person could be wealthy. Why is one child sick and dying and another lives for 100 years? Why does one child live in luxury and another live in a part of the world where he is starving? Especially, if we believe that we only have one life to live. Who decides all of this? Is it fate? Is it just pure luck?

I did my research and realized that if we did have many opportunities to live, or have many lives, it would make sense because we are just experiencing different journeys. In one journey we can be rich and in another life, the reverse could be true, and we could be poor. We could be healthy in one life and sickly in another. We need to experience dark and light, so we are given different lives.

I began to study reincarnation and attempted to understand better why a being has a certain path in this life with certain experiences. Every physical life is a cycle full of experiences, events, and learnings designed to clean up our past karma. Imagine that we are an infinite soul, and we're told to go free and experience all possibilities. When we become complete, we could go back. We become complete by learning good and bad, learning from the consequences of our choices, and by growing and evolving through universal living. We create less negative karma for ourselves, learn how to better control our actions, and finally live in total peace with love for all. Buddha and Jesus lived that life because of the level of their soul journeys, to them, everything was love and joy.

I invite you to imagine the whole world being one; imagine a big ocean, and you are the wave coming along. The wind is pushing you and sometimes changing your shape. Finally, you head to the shore, then you go back out to the ocean, starting over and over, again and again. We are all one, like the ocean, doing our own soul's cycle of waves.

If we look at the origin of it all, we start with being born. As a little baby, you are innocent. Have you ever looked into a baby's eyes and just felt the wonder inside of them? If you feel this, you can imagine that they are 100 percent free and not conditioned or tainted yet by society's beliefs. You can see in their eyes the purity and innocence of their soul. The baby has not been conditioned yet into a three-dimensional world. As the child grows, we warn the child to be cautious, so it won't get hurt; we teach them about the world and how to speak, and teachers support their left brain to get more knowledge and understanding. Slowly they start to lose their wonder. As a child begins becoming a kid, they get to see more and more structural patterns in school, at home, and in society. The kid begins to become alert and cautious not to upset people or disrupt things. So, the kid starts to have negative vibrations, somewhere inside them is a sense of fear that something could go wrong. Then, the kid starts wanting to be in a more controlling position, rather than in a position of allowance. Eventually, the kid grows older and becomes his own judge of situations with all his negative beliefs in the background. This goes on and on, and until the kid is a grown-up conditioned with controlling fears, and he has forgotten what it was like just to relax and enjoy the moment like that baby he once was. This happens to us all.

Our belief systems are embedded into us from early childhood, and our culture perpetuates these beliefs. If you start questioning your belief systems, you come closer to what your values are. Now that we have more information; we don't have to believe what our parents believe or what society believes, and actually if you look inside, you will be able to feel from your intuition what is right and what is wrong for you. Your truth is unique, and it comes from your life experience and learnings. Don't fall victim to other people's beliefs; maybe someone believes in karma or mantras, but if that's not true for you, you don't have to believe it. Having said all of this, I can say for a fact that the fundamental teaching or answer from our souls is the way of love, being in peace and harmony with yourself and the world around you. Love is always the answer.

This feeling of unconditional love is in all of us. You will discover it when you go inside of yourself. If you are ever overwhelmed by the roller coaster of life, just take a moment and go inside and find your home. And don't judge the roller coaster, remember if you don't know darkness, how can you know the light?

To help you look into what your purpose is during this roller coaster we call life, here is a little tool:

Look and examine the following:

1. Who you are: your name, your childhood, your good and bad qualities, and your belief systems?

2. What type of occupation, trade, or job do you have or want to have?

3. Who are/would be the clients or people you help?

4. What do these clients want or need from you?

5. What effect do you have on your clients or people who want something from you?

As you can see, it is more about what others get from your best, rather than what you get from theirs. You didn't come to this life for personal gain; you came to this life to pass on your gift to others. This is going to be fun and exciting, and I know in the end you will find yourself a calmer person with great knowledge of yourself, better control of your thoughts and emotions, and a higher vibration toward your focused desires.

## CHAPTER 4

# Wisdom and Concepts

There are so many questions and so many answers. I will try to briefly explain certain important concepts so you can have a choice to go deeper into each subject based on what resonates with you.

You must try to be open to all of the concepts; read through them and afterwards reevaluate which ones you like and want to go further into. There is so much information available on each of these items, and you can focus deeper on one of them on your own.

Do yourself a big favor and not try to pick a point here and there. Go through the brief explanations of each concept and get the overall picture. That way in a later chapter, we can put the concepts to use to help you create a calmer, better life.

The main key is to be an observer and not a judge. Learning new things in life takes courage, and it all starts by becoming an observer first. Then you can digest the information and apply it to your life. Otherwise, your old belief system will hold you back from gaining knowledge.

For example, there is the concept of God. God has different meanings for different people. I believe in God as the universe or ultimate creator full of love. You have to find your truth.

Knowledge is the number one tool to awakening your beliefs; there are many questions that need answers. When you read through these concepts keep an open mind, you may have judgments or preconceived notions, but just put them to the side for now and watch and read with an open mind and heart.

## GOD

The first thing I truly learned was that God exists. In essence, I learned that God is everything and everywhere.

Simply said, God is "all." God is the universe itself. When you find God on the inside, you will find him everywhere else, but if you look only on the outside, you may never find him because he starts inside of you. Actually, everything on the outside is a reflection of what you are on the inside. For example, if you are optimistic on the inside you see the world as full of opportunities, but if you are negative and pessimistic on the inside, you will only see the world as a place full of negative obstacles. You are part of God, experiencing physical life at this time. So, you need to look inside yourself to find him.

God is in your spirit, your higher self. Your higher self is the creator of your soul. God gave us the opportunity to come to this Earth in a physical form, so our soul can learn lessons and ultimately come back to the source. God gives us the opportunity to experience love. We keep coming back in a physical form until we have fully realized that we are love. Then, we go back to God, our source.

Think of God as the ocean, your higher self as a bucket of water from that ocean, and your soul as a cup of water from the bucket. All of them are connected. God is invisible in that cup, but he is the source. He manifested the visible universe through us. As a cup of water, you cannot know you are part of a bucket, and as a bucket, you cannot know you're also the ocean. But that's how it works.

Here are a few stories to give you a sense of God's place with us.

One late rainy night in the middle of nowhere an old lady got a flat tire. All of a sudden, an old car stopped, and a scraggly looking guy came out. He could see the fear in the lady, so from afar he said, "Ma'am, just sit in your car and relax. I will fix your tire. My name is Bryan Anderson. If you could just open your trunk, I will take care of the rest."

She opened her trunk and he started fixing her tire for her. While he was working on the tire, she started a conversation with him, and when he was done, she asked, "How can I repay you?"

He said, "I don't need payment. God wanted me to do this. Since you were stuck here in the rain, it was the kind thing to do." She kept insisting on paying him, and eventually, he said, "If you want to pay me back, the next time you see someone in need, give them your support as I did for you."

The old lady continued driving and eventually, she stopped for a cup of coffee at a diner. At the diner was a pregnant waitress, who was very kind and took great care of the old lady. After her coffee, the old lady thought about Bryan and what he said to her, so when the bill came, she gave the waitress a $100 bill. When the waitress went to get her change she came back, and the old lady was gone. At the table there was $400 under a napkin that had written on it: "Here is some money to help you with your baby." The waitress saw the napkin and immediately started to cry. She went home, got into bed, and thanked God. Then she turned and kissed her husband, and said to him, "Bryan Anderson, God did it again."

Another story goes:

A man walking through the forest saw a fox that had lost his legs. He noticed that a tiger was bringing him food. The man was amazed by God's grace, so he decided to test God. He lay in the forest waiting for days for food. After a week or so of waiting, he was at death's door and God came to him and said "You have taken the wrong path. Follow the example of the tiger, not the disabled fox."

Here is a final story:

> A man was having a dream, and in this dream, he was walking on the beach with God. Behind them were their footsteps, and every footstep represented moments or memories in his life. It was clear to him in this dream that God was walking with him through his life and was always there for all of it. Once in a while, he could only see his own footsteps behind him, and these were the times when he felt the saddest or desperate in his life. So he asked God, "Why did you leave me to walk alone during these times?"

> God said, "My son, I love you so much, I did not leave you alone. I was carrying you through those times. That's why you only see one pair of footsteps."

Imagine a playground with all possible toys and things to do. Imagine you send your child inside this fenced playground to play. He is free to play with whatever he wishes while you are outside the fence watching your child. He goes and plays one game, then another. He has fun. He laughs; he cries; he jumps; he falls. But you are on the outside watching, making sure he is safe. You are also feeling good because your kid gets to be happy, he is learning different games, gaining different experiences, and you know that at the end of the day he will come back to you, and you can clean him and pamper him and make sure he knows how much you love him.

Our Earth life is very similar. No matter what happens, God loves us and pampers us when we meet him again. Our faith and devotion will help us to get through all the bumps and bruises and cries on the playground.

God wants you to get what you truly want. The key word is truly, which also includes unconscious and subconscious desires. Even if what you want is bad, God will let you experience that because that's your path. You will either learn from those consequences in this life or the next.

When we speak about God, it's the most important fundamental aspect of who you are. God is our creator and all-knowing being. So, seeking God is the essence of seeking the truth of who we are, why we are here, and where we are going.

## FAITH

Faith can be defined as knowing through intuitive perception, stepping into the unknown, and believing that the event or desire will be there.

Faith is not stepping into the dark; it is stepping into the light.

Faith is the deep trust in God, life, universal intelligence, and your soul. This trust is much deeper and beyond your mind. It is inside of all of us; we just have to feel it. The mind deals with your beliefs only; you have to go deeper than your beliefs to find faith. Your faith is actually your power.

Faith is also the end of all fear, realizing that you are not just the body, but you are actually connected to God.

Faith is the bridge between thinking or believing and trusting. It is the confidence and validity of something before the proof is manifested physically.

## SOUL

I began to understand the difference between my body, my thoughts, my five senses, my dreams, and my intuition. My intuition comes from a different place inside of me.

I believe that many times in my life, "guardian angels" came to warn me or protect me from making very bad choices or from accidents that could have happened to me. They came in a voice that I can only call my intuition.

I started to become very curious about whether I had a soul and what function the soul plays in my life. I came to the conclusion that my intuition is my soul speaking to me.

Most of us believe that we have a physical body and our personality governs the way we think, feel, and behave. So, we conclude that that is all there is.

The truth is:

Our spirit (the essence of us and pure energy connected to God) is housed in a series of bodies.

Our soul (the vehicle for the spirit to express our mortal value through our conscious and intuition) is the original form of ourselves.

Our personality is the vehicle for our spirit and soul to express itself and learn.

1.) **GARY ZUKAV:** "The soul is that part of you that existed before you were born and that will exist after you die. It's the highest, most noble part of yourself that you can reach for."

2.) **VANA VANSANT:** "The soul, I believe, is the fingerprint of God that becomes a physical body. I believe that. It's the fingerprint... it's unique to everybody"

3.) **DEEPAK CHOPRA:** "The soul is the core of your being. It is eternal. It doesn't exist in space/time. It's a field of infinite possibilities, infinite creativity. It's your internal reference point with which you should always be in touch."

4.) **DEVON FRANKLIN:** "The soul is the spirit. It is the connecting line to God. I believe the soul is where the Holy Spirit resides. I believe that it is literally, you know when you pick up the phone and then you have your 4G or 5G network? The soul is the 4G network right to heaven to me."

5.) **SARAH BAN BREATHNACH:** "The soul is the spiritual essence of who we really are."

6.) **DANIEL PINK:** "The soul is, I think, our capacity to see that our lives are about something more than simply the day-to-day, and that we're here for a purpose. It could be connected to religion or not, but that there is a purpose of your being here."

7.) **DEBBIE FORD:** "To me, the soul is a part of us that never dies. It's who we are at our core. And it carries all the messages and the lessons that we've learned in the past and will carry all the lessons and the messages that we will carry into the future."

8.) **ECKHART TOLLE:** "The soul is your innermost being. The presence that you are beyond form. The consciousness that you are beyond form, that is the soul. That is who you are in essence."

9.) **MICHAEL SINGER:** "The indwelling consciousness that watches the mind come and go. That watches the heart come and go, the emotions of the heart. And watches the world pass before you. You, the conscious, the consciousness, the center of being, are the soul."

10.) **WAYNE DYER:** "The soul is the birthless, deathless, changeless part of us. The part of us that looks out from behind our eyes and has no form. The soul is infinite, so there is no in or out of it. It is everywhere. There's no place that it is not."

11.) **MARIANNE WILLIAMSON:** "For me, it's the truth of who we are. The light, the love, which is within us, goes by different names, but the truth of us. Michelangelo said when he got a statue that he would go to the quarry and get a big piece of marble, and the way he imagined it, God had already created the statue and his job was just to get rid of the excess marble. So that's what we're like. Inside is the being that God has already created. Some call it the Christ, Buddha, mind, the shekinah, the light, the soul. And our job is to get rid of this excess, useless fear, thought forms of the world that actually hide the light of the soul."

12.) LLEWELLYN VAUGHAN-LEE: "The soul is a divine part of our self. It is our divine nature. It is a part of us that is one with God. Everybody has a soul. It is the immortal internal part of us. It never dies. It's immortal. It belongs to God."

13.) JEAN HOUSTON: "I believe that the soul is the essence of who and what we are. I personally believe that it transcends our leaving this mortal coil. And I think it comes with codes and possibilities, and the next layers of whom and what we may yet be. It is often a pain in the neck because it says, 'wake up. It's time to wake up. Don't go to sleep.' I think it is also the lure of our becoming. That's what I think the soul is."

I believe that the whole universe has consciousness and all things in physical or nonphysical forms have consciousness, and we are all part of a larger universal consciousness that is immortal and is part of God. As we come to Earth life, our soul joins our earthly personality, which contains our mind and body. When we die, our soul (consciousness) rejoins the universal consciousness, the spirit of God, and our higher self. It is important to learn the agenda of our soul while we are on this Earth. There are events and experiences that will take place and lessons to be learned. Also, our soul comes with a gift to give to Earth; we need to find out what this gift is that we are to give.

## WHAT IS A SOUL?

Each thing in this universe has a soul. Plants and inanimate objects have souls. Animals share group souls. Humans have an individual soul. We should say our soul started its physical journey as a mineral, then it became a plant/tree, then an animal, before incarnating as a human.

Your soul resides in a pyramid shape in your chest; the apex resting on the bottom of your throat, and the base resting on the top of your diaphragm.

Your soul is the electric energy flowing through your body; without the electricity, your body is a light bulb with no light.

Your soul is not only the engine of your life, but it also embodies why things exist within the human species.

So, what happens to you when you die? Do your personality and soul also die? But if that is true, then why is there so much proof that the body remains but the soul moves on? Does this mean your soul immortal?

Dr. Duncan Mac Dougall proved that the body loses weight at the time of death. According to his findings, when a person dies, their body releases 21 grams of weight. He determined this in 1907, and for many, this is proof that the soul does exist.

Knowing the soul exists, it is important to understand the soul. There are degrees of soul consciousness, not all humans are equally aware of their souls, and souls have no beginning and no end. Some souls are even older than others.

Before the soul decides to return or incarnate, it agrees to perform certain tasks, such as raising a family, being a creator or artist, being a soldier, teacher, or a writer, or even having a disability. All of your experience will allow your soul to fulfill its contract for this life.

Your soul also came to this Earth to learn lessons; these lessons are learned through your experiences on Earth. Your soul has a specific gift to give to this Earth. In conjunction, it is also here to pay its karmic debts, balance its energy, and evolve and change into the best version of itself.

The lessons your soul must learn are the consequences that you have created from your present or past lives. To satisfy your karma, you face the consequences. Note that facing your consequences doesn't mean that you have learned your lesson. You will only learn when you decide to take the time to feel the lesson, feel the emotion of the lesson, see the consequence, be grateful to the lesson, and send light. It's like a self-fulfilling prophecy.

I am sure some of you have asked, "why does this keep happening to me?" Learning comes when you have the courage to understand your mistakes and you decide not to be in these situations ever again; it is the result of being grateful and thankful to that lesson, not ignoring it, brushing it off, shoving it under the carpet, or feeling anger and hate. If you run or ignore the lessons, they will repeat themselves over and over again until you realize the importance of this lesson. Once you feel the lessons, then your soul is satisfied and will move on to the next lessons.

You have a choice to live as you wish but no matter what, these lessons that your soul needs to experience will pop up sooner or later. That is why the old saying goes "you do not know what life has coming for you the next day." If you think these events in your life are an accident, think again. For example, if someone owes you money for work you have done, but they are telling you they will not pay, making you angry, then maybe you have done something similar to another person in the past. Now, it is your turn to feel the consequence of karma. So calm down, feel the anger, thank karma for the experience that you are going through, make a deep decision that you will never do the same to others going forward. You must send love to the other party, ask for forgiveness to all the people that you may have done that same thing to, and bless all the people that are in the same situation as you are. Take this time to feel inside you the lesson you were supposed to learn.

You need to learn to slow down and observe so that your soul's lessons can be learned. Things happen for a reason. The reason is that there is a lesson to be learned. Do not try to be intellectual and try to find solutions with your mind. Your mind works with your thoughts and logic; your soul feels the emotion inside your heart. Many people tell you to listen to your heart and not your mind. The reason for this is that your heart speaks from your soul, and your soul uses your body in this earthly life to learn and feel the lessons that it needs to learn. To avoid the experience from happening again, your soul needs to complete the learning of the lesson; that means you must do the above exercise, as outlined in the example, so your soul will be satisfied.

Your soul is the entire novel of your being; your present life is a chapter. As your soul rejoins your higher self, it takes a look at the last chapters of past life and decides what you need to go through in the next chapter of the next life. When your soul goes back to your higher self, it's like being on a holiday in heaven. Your soul gets filled with love again, then looks at the situation and realizes it's time for some more work to be done.

Before we reincarnate into this new journey, which will include the lessons and experiences for the school of the evolution of the soul and working towards the completion of the circle of our consequences (karma), your soul receives advice from your heavenly guides; they will review the past lives and advise you with sets of lessons to be learned in the next lifetime. You then choose the place and situation to most help you to learn these lessons that you are to experience. This includes the location, condition of your life, and YOUR PARENTS. Because of the choice of these parents, they are the best to provide you the condition needed for your experiences to occur. Furthermore, you choose the place that you are born, the economic condition you will live in, the race you will be, and the religion you will follow. These are pre-calculated and chosen, so when you come back to Earth school, you will have the best opportunity to experience all the lessons set for your soul. So, please, next time you see another being, do not judge them; instead, understand that this is their journey and present life, bless them as who they are, and be kind regardless.

Most of us think that our parents brought us to this world; little do we know, we are the ones who chose them. They truly are our parents, and we should love and respect them, as they were our soul's choice. We must continue to care for them and take responsibility to make sure we do all we can as they get older. Life is a circle; your parents take care of you as you are young, and you take care of them as they get old. The same effort and love that they give you when you are a child is the same effort and love you should give as they get old. Some children believe their parents always owe them and must take care of them. While it is true, parents always love their kids and will do everything to help them, the obligation of raising kids is with parents, and the obligation of taking care of older parents is with kids. If either side ignores their responsibility, there will be consequences.

The language of your soul is love. So, when you ask your soul questions, it feels as if the answers are coming from your heart. When you ask your heart or soul something, the answer is almost always positive, coming from a loving space inside of you. The answer is usually not something like "punch the idiot."

If we approach all things from a soul's point of view, rather than a mind's point of view, we can open unlimited potentials and opportunities that we could have never imagined from our mind and its limited beliefs and past experiences. Our soul has experienced so much more than our mind, so we should use our soul as an important tool to navigate life.

The true home for your soul is in the non-physical world with your higher self.

## SOUL AGE:

There are seven levels of the soul: Infant, Baby, Young, Mature, Old, Transcendental, and Infinite.

1. **INFANT SOUL:** This soul age asks, "Where am I? And who are you?" In this stage, the soul is trying to cope and survive.

2. **BABY SOUL:** This soul age understands, "These are the rules, and they must be followed. I need someone to tell me where I fit in and what should I do." These people live a routine life, doing things like going to work, attending church on Sunday, or playing sports. This soul age could be comparable to living in small towns in America.

3. **YOUNG SOUL:** This soul age believes, "I can have it all; it's me against you, and I'm going to win." They do not pursue what they like; they pursue what they believe will create success. They want to live where successful people live. They are productive, industrious, and innovative. They can also be competitive, pushy, self-righteous, and excessively materialistic.

4. MATURE SOULS: This soul age knows, "My life is intense, real, and dramatic, but there is something missing from my life." They are emotionally open and relationship-oriented. Their soul age is very balanced. They can also be hard on themselves, intense, and neurotic, and they can have success and crises.

5. OLD SOULS: This soul age says, "You are who you are, and I am who I am. I am tired of this game; I can see the bigger picture and I want to live by it." They perceive themselves and others as a part of something greater, understanding of the connection existing among all beings. They are easy-going, caring, laid back, and spiritually aware. They have a sense of love for everyone. They are also arrogant and can be weird or lazy.

6. TRANSCENDENTAL SOULS: They rarely reincarnate on this Earth, and if they do reincarnate, historically, they come as a teacher or guru to help humanity.

7. INFINITE SOULS: The souls are a representation of God and love itself, like Christ or Buddha.

You may see many similarities between a soul age above and yourself. It is important to know your soul age, so you can study for your soul age and find out where your soul is on its journey. Knowing can also help you relax because you will understand how much life is still ahead of you, and you can determine the right choices to make the road shorter and more pleasant.

## THE DIFFERENT LIFE ROLES: WHICH IS YOUR ROLE?

*Scholar, Sage, Priest, Server, Artisan, Warrior, King*

Your higher self has a basic plan for each lifetime that it sets out to fulfill. The main parts of your life, like your personality, body type, and astrology, are all chosen in order to make this plan possible. In this life plan, you also play a role; you can inquire inside what your role is.

*How do I determine someone else's role?*

First, determine whether they look ordinary, exalted, or natural. If they have an ordinary everyday look, they are most likely an artisan, server, or a warrior. If they stand out and look special, they are exalted, then most likely they are a sage, priest, or king. If they appear natural, then they are scholars. If you are in doubt, you can look into their eyes. Eyes tell a great deal about a person's soul age, role, and other qualities. It is important for you to know that you will have the same ROLE in all of your journeys and soul ages, so knowing your Role will help you to understand your actions and reactions toward everything. There are many good books for your understanding of your Role.

## Scholar Role:

Scholars make up less than 15 percent of the population. They are naturally full of experiences and knowledge.

The positive attributes of scholars include being well orderly, well organized, coherent, formal, disciplined, audacious, fearless, brave, venturesome, logical, thoughtful, objective, well balanced, and grounded.

The negative attributes of scholars include being secluded, isolated, withdrawn, conceptual, abstract, grimy, grubby, unassertive, submissive, and arrogant.

Scholars are well-educated, experienced, and knowledgeable people. They focus on their different experiences and gain knowledge from these experiences, which is why they are known as the walking encyclopedia of human experiences. They are full of intuitional knowledge, and they gain more understanding by connecting to their intuition and hands-on experiences. They devote themselves to gaining all experiences from a task, no matter how productive the task may be. They seek experience, adding present and past life experiences to their library of knowledge.

How they go about gaining the knowledge of an experience is different than other Roles. To a scholar, every task is as important as any other task, whether it be small or big, good or bad. To a scholar, the feeling of the experience is fulfilling.

Scholars are reserved and unattached, and most of them meditate regularly. Because they play the role of an observer, they tend not to engage in any act of others; they are non-confrontational.

Scholar's eyes are neutral and have a special emotional demeanor. You can find them in all walks of life, mostly doing one thing to master it and gain all the needed experience. They may be an iron metal man, a comedian, or a surgeon. They seek all there is to gain knowledge in one field to add to their walking library of life. They love to share experiences that they have with others, and you will always find them around books or informational sources. They will go to the extreme to gain knowledge. They compromise with all people and avoid conflict.

## Sage Role:

Sages are less than 10 percent of the population. Sages are articulate and express their thoughts and emotions.

The positive attributes of sages include being detail-oriented, funny and entertaining, curious about everything, intrigued, loving, charming, knowledgeable, and smart.

The negative attributes of sages include being attention-seeking, causes emotional discomfort, excessively loud, grandiloquent, magniloquent, misleading, ambiguous, conceited, and opinionated.

Sages are the main vocal translators of the world; they are the main resources of the information needed to make the correct changes in our life. They are authors and teachers and public speakers who can inspire us. They give us wisdom in a fun and loving way. Their teaching ability helps all.

**Priest Role:**

Priests make up less than 10 percent of the population. Priests are inspiring and very concerned for the sufferings or misfortune of others.

The positive attributes of priests include being humane, compassionate, promote human welfare, feed the hungry, encourage and protect others, and cure and heal others.

The negative attributes of priests include being unreasonable, illogical, thoughtless, inconsiderate, unkind, and insensitive.

Priests have a way of making us calm and at ease. Their inspiration will drive us to seek evolution and positive outcomes. They help us see the difference between fear and love.

Priests are here to heal us, and their energy can help us become at ease and calm. They are sympathetic and compassionate, which is seen in their features and their voices. They make you feel as if you are in a loving environment; you can feel their love, your love, and your soul. They have a special connection with you. Their teaching mostly involves the higher self and teachings of the Universal Law.

**Server Role:**

Servers are among the highest percentage of the world's population. Servers make up over 25 percent of the population. They are very inspirational and ordinal.

The server's positive attributes include being concerned, friendly, inspiring, able, adept, knowledgeable, maneuvering, and controlling.

The server's negative attributes include being feeling victimized, frustrated, domineering, disenfranchised and seeing themselves as a victim.

Servers are confident, hard, and capable workers, who perform a valuable service for all. They help us with our needs, and they put them before their own. They set an example of helping as serving as a role model.

## Artisan Role:

The main essence of Artisan is creativity, wanting to create new things and an inventiveness that creates new things. Artisans have a high-frequency role, and they are flexible in life.

The artisan's positive attributes include being original, eccentric, imaginative, gamesters, spontaneous, innovative, mood creator, and different.

The artisan's negative attributes include being irresponsible, self-indulgent, moody, impulsive, bizarre, and more emotional than other roles.

They approach their life as a playground for activities and creativity.

Michelangelo is a good example of an Artisan. They are creative in all aspects of life: clothing, art, expression, etc. They strongly relate to music, style, creative ideas, moods, and new conceptual schemes.

## Warrior Role:

Warriors consist of less than 20 percent of the population, and they are convincing, persuasive, and articulate.

The positive attributes of warriors include being focused and energetic, on task, love to take on new tasks, proud individuals, and true survivors.

The negative attributes of warriors include being direct, devious, narrow-minded, quick to temper, angry, seek fights and arguments, unforgivable individuals, brutal, pushy, and at times violent.

Warriors are here to get things done in society. They make things happen; they set goals and focus to get accomplish those goals. They believe the world is their playground to explore. They know what they want, and they know how to get it by being persistent.

## King Role:

Kings are less than 5 percent of the population. Kings are controlling and take action.

The positive attributes of kings are leaders, good-natured, charming, fascinating, dominant, superior, powerful, despotic, and autocratic.

The negative attributes of kings are rude, inflexible, impolite, demanding, at times ruthless, narrow-minded, uncompromising, rigid, small-minded, and unsympathetic.

Kings do not look cold, thin, and worried; they look strong and determined. Their eyes are focused and cold; they radiate energy and are full of authority. They command loyalty.

King's eyes are focused and unwavering. Their face is excessively thin and angular, a long gaunt face.

Kings speak with commanding authority, and they stay with a task until they become completely skillful at it.

Kings are on top of their profession and sometimes hold thrones. They are fixers of all problems and lead people to take positive action. They delegate all portions of a big task to skilled individuals to get the job done.

# REINCARNATION

The word "carna" means fresh; incarnation is the process of a soul entering into a physical human body, and reincarnation means the soul is repeatedly entering various bodies life after life. We are all spirits, and by incarnating we come to Earth for different reasons. Some come to explore; some come to help, and some come to simply enjoy the physicality of being alive in a body. We keep coming back to learn lessons, and if we don't learn them in one life, we come back to learn them again. We also come back to complete unfinished business, like actions we took, such as words or thoughts that may have caused suffering or harm to others. So, in these lives, we create karma that we need to clear in our next lives. Our soul needs its evolution; our soul must go through all the soul ages and levels to be completed.

When we learn our lessons and "re-take" our "mistakes," we complete a portion of our karma, and we learn. Also, people we meet and see usually have some karma with us. When we become more knowledgeable and have more understanding of what the right thing to do is, we bring ourselves into a higher vibration than before, and we learn much faster, thus speeding up the process and not having to reincarnate as much.

The reason why we don't remember our past lives is so we don't use the information to control our current life or overshadow our choices. Once we understand this process, we can see, for example, why one person may be rich and another poor. Maybe in a previous life, it was the other way around. Sometimes you meet someone, and you feel like you have known them forever or you have met them before. These deep intuitive feelings come from our past lives.

Hindus found that death was like a withdrawal of electricity from your living body. So, when we die the electricity leaves our body, but like a light bulb that goes out, the electricity doesn't die. So, when we die our body dies, but the electricity, our soul, leaves the body and goes into the ocean of cosmic energy, getting closer and closer to God in each life and death.

How much time each reincarnation takes varies widely. The shortest from person to person is 10 months, and the longest is 800 years. The average is about 40 years. Less developed souls, who thirst for a new body, won't spend long in the life in between life.

Medical stats show that a fertilized egg has less than a 27 percent chance of surviving in the first six weeks of pregnancy and a 93 percent chance of surviving afterward. Most souls do not get involved with a fetus until close to birth, and some even come in during the birth process itself. So, the belief that abortions kill the soul is 90 percent false.

In ancient Greece, Plato wrote that reincarnating souls drink from the river of forgetfulness, and once the soul drinks this water, it forgets everything about the afterlife. In the Jewish faith, they believe that an angel of forgetfulness touches us on our upper lip, making a little indentation just before we are born and erasing all the memory of our heavenly home and reasons for choosing this life.

## KARMA

Karma is an impersonal universal teacher of love and responsibility. When you understand this, then you will be less likely to react from your ego with anger, outrage, judgment, or righteousness.

Karma exists for man, so that he may learn from its workings the wisdom of returning from multiplicity to unity. Actions performed by your own will in this life are called "purushaker," and actions performed by the influence of habits established in past lives are called "samskara."

There are many different sayings related to karma: "what goes around comes around," "you reap what you sow," "live by the sword and die by the sword," and "an eye for an eye."

All of the sayings mean the same thing: what we do will come back to us with an equal consequence sooner or later. It's impossible to escape from this law. By giving love, you'll receive love back; by giving pain, you will receive pain back. Karma is not God's punishment to us; it is a process of dealing with the consequences of our actions from both the past and the present. So, we have a total choice in creating our future. We have a choice to create from the loving side of us (our soul) or from the reactive part of us (our ego).

We face our karma to learn lessons, so we must not act like a victim of the circumstances, using them to grow instead. We need to learn to start responding instead of reacting. When we respond, we learn how the situation can help us, and, eventually, we can be grateful for what is happening in our lives. Remember, the ultimate goal is always to love; love will always be the answer to your karmic experiences.

You will reap what you sow; if you want to be loved, start loving others who need your love. If you expect others to be honest with you, then start being honest yourself. Whatever you want others to be, be it yourself first. Give what you need. Remember the energy that you put out will attract the same energy; if you put out negative energy, you will receive the same negative energy. If you put out positive energy, you will receive the same positive energy. Karma works like a magnet, attracting similar things, so if your mind tells you that your life sucks but you start sending positive energy and gratefulness into the world, soon you will be attracting the same positive energy and gratefulness into your own life. You cannot change the past and what has been done to you. Know that it was a lesson to feel and learn and let go. You can only control the "now", and your "now" will manifest what is ahead. A positive attitude, plus love, will benefit you and help you become wise.

## PERSONALITY AND BODY

Your personality includes:

1. Your physical body and five senses

2. Your intellect—the ability to think and reason

3. Your emotions

4. Your intuitional structure—as you become multi-sensorial, you will become more intuitive

Personality is a part of you that was born with your body on a certain day and will die with your body on a certain day. Your personality experiences different emotions, and it is with you all the time. You cannot hide it while you're alive, but based on the experiences you have and the lessons you learn, you can change your personality. So, when you heal your negative emotions, your soul heals through your personality, and you develop.

Your body includes different levels:

1. The physical body and five senses

2. The astral body (emotional body)—when you're asleep or deep in mediation your emotional body detaches from your physical body

3. Your mental body, also known as your thinking body

4. Your spiritual body, your soul and spirit

When we die, that is the end of all pain and suffering; at death, our soul departs from our body to form the astral body.

# BRAIN

What does the brain do? What are the functions of the right and left sides of the brain?

The brain is the instrument used to process thoughts; it is the greatest cluster where neurons are concentrated in the body, so it is a huge center of intelligence. Your brain processes 400 billion bits of information per second, but we are only aware of 2,000 bits of all of this information, and those 2,000 bits are only about the body, environment, and time.

The left side of the brain deals with logic. Facts, patterns, science, and numbers are handled by the left side. This is the side we are using most in our daily life. Your soul gives you inspiration through your left brain.

Your right side of the brain rules your conscious mind. It is the thinking and processing side, which also deals with emotions. Intuition, creativity, empathy, symbols, images, risk-taking, religion, and philosophy.

The philosophy of working hard to get rich is from the old days. It's important to work hard towards your goals, but it's also important to allow intuition and creativity to come from your right side. Children have been studied, and it's been shown that from ages 2 to 4, kids are much more intelligent than the kids around age 7. This is because we have conditioned them with school and structure, and we increase the capability of their left brain and not their right brain. There are many ways to improve the usage of the right side of your brain and to tap into the unlimited universal consciousness. In the future, we can get into how to do that and how to improve your creativity and intuition.

Your mind is your brain in action. We can measure the efficiency of your brain by studying your mind. If the brain is the intelligence or instrument for processing thoughts, and the mind does what the brain wants it to do, then what is improving the brain? The answer is your consciousness. Consciousness is not the body, brain, or mind; consciousness is what guides the brain to create the mind.

So, if we can access our consciousness beyond our body, environment, and time, then we open the door to the universal intelligence that governs everyone on the planet's intelligence. This is the same intelligence that governs the entire world. This intelligence governs our body as well; it created the amazing system of cells that makes our heart pump blood and keeps us alive. There are two ways to make a connection with the brain. The first is through knowledge; every time we learn a new thing, we are making a connection with our brain. The second is through experience; every time we experience something new, all of our five senses are picking up the information and sending it to the brain. Our brain turns this into an emotion or a feeling. So, if we put our brain through something over and over again, it becomes a habit, and we can create new habits based on how we want to live our lives.

# MIND

What is your mind?

The mind is nothing except your thoughts. You can see your mind by sitting back and watching your thoughts. Watch the words in your mind float in front of you, giving you a visual of your thoughts. This is seeing your mind. Thoughts can have language and pictures, what you see when you are in stillness is your mind; in meditation, you can even try to separate your mind from your body.

The mind can become a hostage of the body because of the drama created by your thoughts and feelings. In order to change, you just have to ask, "what do I need to be happy? What do I need to change?" When you ask these questions, the front lobe of the brain taps into greater intelligence.

You can ask these questions over and over, especially during meditation, so you create a habit out of it. When we focus on a single subject or goal, the body, mind, and emotions begin to become quiet. And we start to tap into the front lobe of our brain. This allows us to tap into our higher self.

Usually, when we are approaching an extremely challenging task, we choke or succeed. In front of the brain, above our eye level, there is an emotional center; it's called the prefrontal cortex. If you sit down for 10 minutes and outline the emotions that may arise from approaching an extremely challenging situation, then completely express the fear around this situation, then you are able to freeze your emotional center and use your prefrontal cortex to approach the task with less fear and resistance.

## EMOTION

E - motion = Emotion. Energy in Motion.

Emotions are actually energy, and when you feel them, you are feeling the energy through your body. Another way to describe emotions is indicated by the vibrations that you hold in your body. These vibrations are connected to your thoughts. So for example, if you think you are a loser, this negative thought creates a negative vibration (energy), resulting in a negative emotion or feeling. Energy cannot be destroyed; it can only be transformed into something else. Your emotions are signs from your soul, which allow you to feel what you are going through and to support your changing process in this life.

All beings are made of energy. Energy is a part of a system of light, and an individual's light frequency depends on the level of their soul-consciousness. For example, if you get hurt emotionally and you decide to forgive someone, showing them compassion rather than hate and revenge, your frequency is much lighter, and your consciousness is higher. Positive emotions are light energy, but negative emotions are dark and heavy, so the more you unburden yourself and fill yourself with love, compassion, and kindness, the higher your frequency is. And when you are full of light, you become "enlightened" and fully conscious.

The study of DNA also shows that emotions such as fear, have a wider wave pattern than emotions such as love, which have a tighter wave pattern. So, when we are in a state of love, we can reach more of our DNA, and we are more tapped into more of the universal knowledge that is already inside of us. Our DNA contains all our universal knowledge, but many times we leave the majority of this untapped. So, when we are on a positive frequency, we are more able to be creative, determined, and inspired.

When you approach everything from a position of love, you are sending a higher signal and frequency to people and things. In most cases, you can affect the other person's frequency as well, and, consciously or unconsciously, you make a positive difference in everyone's life.

Most people have a lot of fear inside of them. Some things they may fear are the unknown, not being loved—either from their parents, friends, or society—, or failure. Many people live their lives in fear, and some try to compensate for their fears with food, alcohol, or even drugs. The way to combat this fear is to love, living your life from your heart and soul, speaking the language of love, and, to accept fate, stepping into the unknown and knowing that the universe will make it alright. If you see you are in a space of fear or overcompensation, you just need to create more love in your life and in your being. Changing the frequency is not easy, but with exercises you will learn how to stop the old negative frequency and transition into the present moment, changing your frequency from negative to positive in order to benefit you and others.

Once you realize who you really are, the New Me, then you know that you can have whatever you desire, and as long as your intention is with love towards creation and helping the universe, then it's like going to a huge store with an unlimited amount of money and picking all the things you may desire. This earth with all it has to offer is ours as long as we universally deserve to have what is offered to us. The more grateful we are and the more loving we are, the more we receive good things.

As a being, we have choices to make, any kind of choice good, bad, and ugly. We can make a choice of any kind, as long as we know there are consequences for our choices. In the paragraphs above, we talked about making choices that bring us more joy, happiness, and peace with positive consequences. But not everyone will make positive choices. As an observer, we may see people making negative choices, but it is not our place to correct them or offer advice, unless they ask for help. Their soul must learn its own lesson, and they are the ones who have been given that life. It is their experiences and choices that they created and their karmas that need to be cleared.

There is no need to be judgmental, opinionated, or engaged. We are to be observant, loving, and grateful. We, as beings, have different life stories to experience, and that should be respected.

I used to look at the homeless people with a judgmental view, believing them to be lazy and unwilling to get a job. To me, they were a problem in society, but the New Me realized that there was a soul in their body, experiencing their life and clearing their past karmas. There is no need to judge, so I began sending them love and paid more attention to what I could do to help.

In life everyone makes mistakes, and everyone has circumstances to clear and experiences to learn from.

So, when you are experiencing a bad emotion, you can ask yourself "what is it that I desire? What is it that would be good for my best self?" When you get messages from your soul (emotions), it's important to study them, feel them, and learn from them. Otherwise, they will keep coming back, especially if you try to cover them up or hide them.

If you do not learn the lessons that your soul wants you too, the energy inside of you will snowball and hit you again within seven years. That's how energy works. Remember, you cannot destroy energy, and if you don't fully feel, accept, and change your behavior, it will remain inside of you. Not only will it remain inside of you, but the energy will attract more of the same energy, so you will attract the same situations in your life again and again.

Therefore, we must be aware of our emotions. Awareness simply means you can name the emotion you are feeling.

How do we clear an emotion?

1. Allowing yourself to feel your emotions totally. You must pay attention to the emotions that are to be felt and name the emotions.

2. Feel and notice which chakras the emotions are sitting in.

3. Visualize the emotion as energy. Imagine you are filling a balloon full of this energy/emotion that you feel, and the balloon is located in the chakra the emotion is sitting in. Have the courage to really feel every part of the emotion, allow yourself to experience the pain or anger—whatever is there.

4. Picture a knife. Puncture the balloon with the knife. Feel the energy exploding out of you. Let it all go and vanish into the universe. If you feel an emotion while doing this, like relief, you can also express that.

How do we learn the lessons?

When an event occurs, there is an important lesson associated with it.

Try to avoid the old-fashioned approach about being strong and pushing things under the rug. This tactic can be a temporary solution, but the emotion related to the event will pop up again, eventually, and you will be presented with a similar event. Once you have taken your time and truly cleared the emotion and learned from the experience, then you know the event will not reappear.

How can we gain wisdom when an event takes place?

1. You must be aware of the physical circumstances surrounding the event.

2. You must be aware and clear about your thoughts with respect to the event.

3. You must examine the emotion that you feel from this event and do the emotion clearing exercise from before.

Everyone's lessons are different. Once you clear the emotions around an event, you will have more clarity about what your soul is trying to learn.

# CHAKRAS

Chakras are the energy centers where we store our emotions. Certain emotions sit on different chakras, and there are many methods of clearing your chakras and getting yourself grounded.

The seven chakras are the energy centers in our body that energy flows through. Blocked or stuck energy in our seven chakras can often lead to illness. So, it is important to understand what each chakra represents and what we can do to keep this energy flowing freely.

To understand what each chakra does and represents in our body and to learn how we can have this energy flowing freely here is a short summary of the chakra system.

You develop these chakras during the first eight years of your life.

The first chakra is your root chakra, and it develops from ages 0–1. It represents our foundation and feeling of being grounded.

- Location: base of the spine in tailbone area, represents the material world

- Emotional issues: survival issues, such as financial independence, money, safety, success, being loved, food, and sexuality

The second chakra is the sacral chakra or the navel, and it develops from ages 1–2. It represents our connection and ability to accept others and new experiences.

- Location: lower abdomen, about 2 inches below the navel and 2 inches in

- Emotional issues: Sense of abundance, well-being, pleasure, relationships, trust

The third chakra is the solar plexus chakra; it develops from ages 2–3, and it is our ability to be confident and in control of our lives.

- Location: upper abdomen in the stomach area

- Emotional issues: self-worth, self-confidence, self-esteem, emotions, anger, hopelessness, and feelings of failure

The fourth chakra is the heart; it develops between the ages of 3–4. This is our center to exchange love, both receiving and giving.

- Location: center of the chest just above the heart

- Emotional issues: love, joy, inner peace, compassion, and gratitude

The fifth chakra is the throat chakra, and it develops from ages 4–5. It is responsible for our ability to communicate.

- Location: throat

- Emotional issues: communication, self-expression, self-awareness of feelings, integrity, and honesty

The sixth chakra is the third eye chakra. This develops from ages 6–7, and it's our ability to see the big picture and functions as the center of our intuition and psychic abilities.

- Location: forehead between the eyes

- Emotional issues: intuition, imagination, daydreaming, visualization, wisdom, and the ability to think and make decisions

The seventh chakra is the crown chakra; it develops from ages 7–8, and it's the highest chakra, representing our ability to be fully connected spiritually.

- Location: the very top of the head

- Emotional issues: inner and outer beauty, our connection to spirituality, pure bliss, knowing yourself, and self-trust

## THIRD EYE (PINEAL GLAND)

The third eye is also known as the spiritual antenna. It connects you with a higher level of consciousness while allowing you to be present in your physical body. As mentioned before, it is located in the middle of your forehead. The third eye has been represented throughout history as a pine-cone, or pine cone-shaped object, sticking out of the forehead.

The third eye is known for being/having:

- The sixth chakra

- The seat of the intuition

- Clairvoyance

- Precognition

- Out of body experiences

- The ability to see an aura

- Recognition, imagination, visualization, and extrasensory perception

Learning to activate your third eye will make you more aware of yourself and give you the ability to see reality and truth.

Your third eye can be enhanced with certain foods like lemons, mushrooms, apple cider vinegar, blueberries, poppy seeds, grape juice, clay, cilantro, honey, coconut, and seaweed.

## SOME TIPS FOR GETTING THE MOST OUT OF YOUR THIRD EYE ARE:

1. Remove mercury from your body

2. Eat an organic diet

3. Drink non-fluoridated water

4. Use fluoride-free toothpaste

5. Eat less meat and processed foods

6. Exercise and do yoga

7. Stop watching TV

8. Meditate

9. Use your intuition

## A TECHNIQUE YOU CAN USE TO ENHANCE YOUR THIRD EYE:

- Go to a dark room and sit in a meditation posture or lie down with your arms by your head

- Breathe out through your mouth and observe your thoughts and your breathing

- Don't resist your thoughts; let them flow and pass

- Focus on the tension in your face, neck, and around your ears

- Let go of this tension

- Take a deep breath and hold it as long as possible

- Release your breath and make the sound "thooooooohhhh"

- Repeat 6 times

- On your next deep breath, make sound "Maaaaaaaayyyhhhhhh"

- Repeat 6 times

- Afterwards, close your eyes and roll them backwards towards the third eye

This method takes practice, but after a while, you should be able to open a door to new visions of truth. Eventually, you may be able to see into the past and future.

Opening and enhancing your third eye will enhance your life in many ways, including how you sleep and your sensitivity with your five senses.

## AURA

Everything in the universe is a vibration; every atom, electron, thought, and emotion. All living and non-living objects have an aura.

The energy that is inside of us also reflects on the outside of us. Therefore, our body is surrounded by the same energy field that emanates from every element of our body. The subatomic energy of every element in our bodies creates a field around us. This field or aura is like a halo around the person, from the top of our head going down in circles. The aura field can also be close to our bodies or further away.

Energy thinks and feels; therefore, the aura showing from our energy field can have a unique intensity or color range. You can tell a lot about a person based on their aura, especially from the colors and intensity of the aura above their seventh chakra. Light colors show good intentions, and dark colors show unclear intentions.

You can tell if someone is telling the truth based on their aura because their aura will emanate truth.

Children up to age 5 can see auras naturally. There are well-published methods of reading auras, and this can help you with dealing with people in your everyday life. You cannot change anybody, but you can see their true intentions.

## HEART

The logic and understanding of our five senses come from our minds; the ability to feel our five senses is part of the intellect. The higher order of logic and understating is the ability to meaningfully reflect and feel the soul. This logic comes from our hearts, and it requires you to be very present in order to feel it.

Emotions are energy in motion, and the ability to be aware of these emotions is the first step in feeling your heart.

What you feel reflects what your intentions are. So, being aware of your emotions leads to you being aware of your intentions.

Without an awareness of your emotions, you are not able to experience reverence. Reverence is not an emotion, rather it is a way of being. The path to it is through your heart. In your heart you are perfect. Learn to open your heart and love. Your heart wants to forgive and be grateful, and it's all about allowing yourself to feel emotions, letting go of burdens, and coming back home to your soul.

Your loving heart can always show you the way.

## LOVE & COMPASSION

Love is focusing positively on something or someone. Love is the vibration of appreciation and total non-resistance. When you love yourself, then you are focusing positively on yourself. So, when you don't love yourself, you attract people like you. And if you are not honest with yourself, it is impossible to love yourself.

Love means appreciation. Gratitude and appreciation are two separate things. They are different vibrations. When you are talking about gratitude, you are happy to be where you are at the present moment in comparison to where you were at in the past. Appreciation has a vibration that is in perfect alignment with who you really are; it is in the state and vibration of love. Love allows the source to be in line with you in a state of appreciation.

So, appreciation is the state of enjoyment.

The only question in a relationship is "how to create more love?"

In relationships you should assume that the other is only giving you respect and love, so you should respond in the same way. In relationships, you will have many excuses why you shouldn't give your love or share your love, but if you want to grow and be connected with the higher frequency, you have to keep putting your energy into creating more and more love.

The best thoughts are thoughts of joy; the best words are words of truth, and the best feelings are feelings of love. There is a famous saying, "Good thoughts, good words, and good deeds."

There are no bad people, only people who have made mistakes or need to be guided into love. No one is intrinsically bad. They may act bad or look bad or speak bad, but as a human being, no one is bad. Do not judge others; everyone is living the experience that is set for them from their soul's point of view. Remember, we are all part of the spirit web full of love.

Selfishness cramps and confines the soul of a person. It puts someone in a space of limitation; selfishness defeats its own purpose. Instead of bringing more happiness into your life, it will only bring more misery. Your intention is all about you and what benefits you only, and not others, which goes against why your soul is on this Earth.

Compassion brings you out of your isolation and into a larger world of love. Compassion is difficult because if you don't accept and appreciate a side of yourself, it will be difficult to be compassionate to another. Everyone is your mirror. When you start to see beyond your judgments and people's appearances and behavior, you start to connect with something deeper, and you go into a space of compassion.

## SELF-LOVE

Self-love is very connected to loving others. When you learn to love others, you learn to love yourself, and when you learn to love yourself, you learn to love others. The key is honesty, forgiveness, gratitude, and compassion.

Remember we are all a part of the same web of love; we must love others and ourselves.

This is difficult for some people, who are critical of themselves or do not value themselves. To break this, live your life for one year asking yourself, "What would someone who loves themselves do?" Ask yourself this question every moment, every hour, and every day of your life for that year. Any time you're going to make a decision, no matter how big or small, check yourself with this question. The answer will never be "punch him in the face" or "hurt myself with addiction." It will always be something positive.

Having this mentality creates more love for yourself and others. It is a way to always find a positive solution.

When you ask this question, the answer comes to you immediately from your intuition, from your higher self, and it allows you to open up and love and appreciate you.

## GRACE

Usually people do not experience grace until something shocking happens to them and they really have a look at themselves. Grace is a spontaneous gift from God; it is given to us through our dealings with God.

That's why many spiritual paths promote gratitude. Gratitude helps you to notice the grace in your life, so you can learn to be thankful and appreciate who you are and what is happening around you. Also saying "thank you" aligns you with the grace that comes from the universe. Your soul becomes connected with the divine.

You can never measure someone else's state of grace; the only life you can experience is your own. Never assume that anyone is fortunate or unfortunate because of the way things look from the outside. It's all about how you look at it. For example, in America, you may find a rich young child pissed off with his mother for not getting him the new iPad to play his games, and in India, you may find a poor, young, dirty child smiling and laughing, playing with his friends and being happy just to be in the moment.

## FEAR

The universe, God, or the source is essentially a vibration of love. The opposite vibration of love is one of fear. In order to get to know God and the source, we must get to know the opposite energy. This is known as the principle of contrast. Life is designed to strip the illusion of fear, and in order to do that, we have to face our fears, feel them, and overcome them, so, eventually, we can see that they are just an illusion. This opens us up to feeling and accepting more love.

Fear is always related to the unknown. We are never afraid of something we know. One way to destroy fear is to gain knowledge of everything and every situation around you. Fears are like dreams, and we are able to wake up from these dreams. If you can understand that your soul is creating everything as a lesson for you to grow, then you can be less afraid and be more courageous to change and grow.

Fear is also an anticipation of pain, but fear itself magnifies our pain tenfold. More often than not, the fear of pain is scarier than the pain itself. And when you shift your orientation from being a victim into being a creator of your life, you will feel more powerful and more positive.

Fear can also manifest itself in our social relationships. Most people identify with a certain group of people, and what they don't realize is that fear itself is a big factor in keeping them together with these people. For example, Christians, Jews, African Americans, etc. tend to associate with people in these same groups. Most of the time if you act in a way that seems out of character for this group, you feel a gap or even a lessening of your connection to them. This creates fear, so when your group tells you to behave in a certain way, you do it in order to fit in because you're afraid of the gap.

This is a big reason that people are conditioned the way they are.

Meditation can help a lot with anxiety or fear, but if you are extremely anxious, then meditation will not work, and you must do something about your anxiety first. What can be helpful is to move your body or to share your emotions with a friend or someone you trust. Anxiety comes from not wanting to face a problem or take responsibility for our actions, so we hope that the circumstances change or a miracle happens to avoid dealing with our fears.

When you are afraid of something, try to locate where it is in your body; usually, it's in between your stomach and heart. Once you locate it, focus on it and ask yourself, "is there any reason why I cannot let go of this fear?" Then just say, "I release this fear." Let the universe resolve the situation.

Letting go of fear can take some time, so keep doing the exercise every day for a while until you feel more relaxed.

We go around trying to protect ourselves in a space of fear, but what we do not realize is that this resistance allows our fears to persist and grow. Fear is not your enemy; everyone feels fear, but if you don't accept it, you will act out on your fear or get depressed, which is not good for you. If you try to ignore the fear, it will get bigger; that's how it works. So, when you're scared to accept it and go for love, force yourself to do it in the direction of love and accept your fear. Fear turns into excitement when you are pursuing love.

Being in the state of "allowing" or "allowance" is the highest state of being. Allowing means, you're so clear of negative energy that love and positivity are flowing through you, and your vibrations, thoughts, and feelings are going in a positive direction for you and the world. Being in this state is actually a state of surrender, and if you have thoughts of fear, anger, or resistance comes up, then you need to do something about it so you can come back to being in a space of allowance.

# RESISTANCE

Nobody stays 100 percent positive and focused at all times. We all have subjects in our life that create more resistance inside of us. Usually, this is because we are focusing on the problem rather than the solution.

You have a lot of energy, and if you focus it on what you want, rather than what you don't want, it makes a big difference.

Resistance comes from having negative thoughts; it means you are going against the river. If you flow with the river, then you are in a higher vibration; this is the state of allowance. When you're having positive thoughts, then you are in the flow.

It's difficult to like or love a situation that you don't want or appreciate, but you can change how you feel about the situation or how you deal with it.

This shift in attitude allows you to change inside of you and helps you learn and overcome your resistance.

You can also use your resistance as a motivation to move towards things that scare you or that you want to work on in self-development. If you have resistance towards something, especially something that seems harmless or nice, then it's good to study it and possibly change your outlook from resistance to acceptance.

Just to make it clear, being happy is not about being in denial. It is about focusing on a solution, rather than the problem, and having the courage to accept your difficulties. Being happy and just ignoring your issues can be like putting sugar on poop, so when resistance comes up, have a look at what that is about inside of you and have the courage to search for a positive solution.

## ADDICTION

You cannot really begin to work on your addictive personality until you acknowledge that you are truly addicted. This is not as simple as it sounds; it is not just about stating, "I have an addiction." It's about really feeling that you cannot trust yourself in a certain aspect of your life. Your personality resists this fact because you want to be in control, and if you cannot trust what you feel (the urge to indulge in an addiction), then you are, in fact, out of control. Once you recognize this, then it can no longer be ignored.

You have to change your life and your self-image.

Addiction is based on magnetism and fear. When there is an attraction to something on the outside, you pursue it. This is a part of your personality that is controlled by outside circumstances, and in reality, you think what you are craving will satisfy you, but, in actuality, nothing on the outside can satisfy what you really need.

If you see that you have compulsions and addictions, it is an indication that there is an unconscious aspect of your personality you still need to learn to deal with and understand.

When you experience something called resistance, an uncomfortable feeling, you can try to escape it with drugs or sugar or alcohol.

Eventually, you become dependent on this substance, and you become powerless. The trick is to welcome the resistance; feel it and look at what is behind it. You don't have to be scared of the resistance; in the end, it is just an indication that you need to experience more love or healing. So, instead of putting your energy towards being an addict, put it towards going for more love.

# INTENTION

You create your reality with your intentions. If you can connect to the universal intention, then you are connected to the total universal DNA, which contains all the answers and solutions to all needs.

An intention is a commitment to accomplishing an objective, to creating something that was not there or to continue something that is.

If you truly desire to change the results of something, the change always begins with your intention. If you have conflicting intentions inside of you related to a topic or goal, they will usually cancel each other out. Though it is important to note that if one intention has a stronger vibration, then it may succeed over the other intention.

Your intention is not simply your desire for something to happen; it is also your willingness to make it happen.

To examine your intentions, you can have a look at your attitude towards others. If you are angry, fearful, resentful, or vengeful, then your intentions are to keep people at a distance.

Your intention and attention shape your experiences. Where your attention goes, you go. What you intend, you will manifest through the density of the divine and it will come true.

If you choose to focus on the light in a person and their strengths, then you start functioning on a higher current of energy that is appreciation, acceptance, and love. If you direct your energy into criticism of others with the intention to put them down or disempower them, then you will create negative karma. Your energy and influence radiate from soul to soul. If your intention is to align your personality with your soul, you start moving towards authentic living. Being compassionate with others includes being compassionate with yourself.

To become aware of the relationship between your consciousness and physical reality is important to learn about the law of karma. What you intend is what you become; if you intend to take instead of giving, then you will attract these same kinds of people in your life.

Here are some steps for you to follow when trying to create positive intentions and a happy reality:

1.  Before you speak or act, become aware of your intentions.

2.  Consider the probable consequences of your intentions.

3.  Choose the intention that creates the consequences you desire. Remember to think about what's best for everyone.

4.  Then look at how the experience unfolds. If it doesn't unfold as you wanted or as fast as you would like it to, look at the aspects of your personality that hold different intentions. Once you find them, try to change these aspects or beliefs.

5.  Take full responsibility for your life. Stop playing the victim of the situation. Realize that everything in your life at this time and moment is exactly what you want because you have created it. You have a lot of unprocessed feelings from your childhood in your subconscious. You also have a lot of pain on the soul level from past lives. These burdens are showing up in your existence now, so it's important to identify them and clean them out, so your energy can increase, and you can start manifesting the life you desire.

## SOME MORE DROPS OF WISDOM:

- Every morning before you get up, remind yourself that you are a cup from the ocean, you and God are one.

- Every time you feel tired, tense, or nervous, exhale deeply, inhale fresh cosmic air, hold your breath and tension in your entire body, then exhale. Do this three times, then enjoy the calmness of your body.

- If you want to heal any part of your body, slowly tense it up then relax it multiple times while you imagine cosmic energy is healing that part of your body. Then, relax your body again.

- If you are very angry, you can take a cold shower and put ice on your medulla.

- Before you go to sleep at night, command your subconscious mind to wake you up at a certain time. You can also command it to get rid of bad habits. Make your commands specific and intense, then relax your mind and flush out all negative energy before falling asleep.

- If your body has excess weight, you should stop and ask yourself why this extra weight is needed. Try to understand the need and why. Once you discover the reason you need this excess weight, you can release it. It may be insecurity or a denial of what your body really needs or wants. It can be a way of punishing itself and saying, "I don't deserve it." Your body wants safety and security, and your body uses fat and food to create it when you're not being nourished emotionally. Look to get nourished, so that you don't need the fat to create security. While you're eating, if you have the thoughts that this food will make you fat, change it to different thoughts, such as this food will nourish you and keep you healthy.

  For example, if you busy yourself with not getting fat, you will not lose weight. You have to be busy with staying healthy and happy.

  It's also important to set goals, which are achievable for you so that you are not constantly frustrated with yourself for not living up to certain expectations. You have to make your relationship with food one more of love, rather than hate.

- Painful emotions are signals from your soul that remind you to stop and experience what you are feeling.

- Your soul gives you two ways of releasing the energy of emotions. The first is by feeling them, and the other is through injury, illness, and physical issues.

- Energy patterns are established the first time when a lesson is presented. This energy pattern causes you to act and think in a certain way every time. The emotion re-emerges, and is called a "seed pattern." The seed pattern is established during the first eight years of your life and is stored in your chakras. This seed pattern will be the basis of your subconscious for the future.

- When you fully feel an emotion from a past experience, you will never get into the same situations again.

- Your soul will attract people who have learned similar lessons as you or people whose learning fits with your own. Sometimes in relationships, you learn different things together.

If you want to learn lessons, it's very important that you look for the power inside of yourself; the lessons are inside of you, and the emotions are inside of you, so you have to create more personal power than wealth or achievements.

## HAPPINESS & HARMONY

The key is understanding that being inwardly happy makes you outwardly happy.

When we are happy, we enjoy life, and when we are unhappy, we are not enjoying life. Often when we are unhappy, we think we should be happy; which usually makes us even more unhappy. This is because on top of being unhappy we are judging where we are at emotionally at the moment, condemning ourselves for not being happy. If we resist our negative emotions, they persist. It's important to remember that instead of being hooked into your negative emotions, you should focus on something positive, that's the key. If you want happiness, go for what makes you happy, feel it in your heart, and go for it.

You will see that just by focusing on something positive, something inside of you will relax about the negative emotions you feel. You will start to accept yourself more and allow yourself to be. Also, when you move your energy enough, then something inside of you will change.

It's also helpful to have some structure, like planning good things to do for yourself daily. Some things you could do include writing lists of daily gratitudes, moving your body and exercising, or having a nourishing meeting with a friend.

Happiness is not something you earn or a point you reach.

Happiness is a state of mind.

Happiness is not something that happens to you; it's something that you need to cultivate and create day after day. Finding your way to being happy again when life brings you challenges will be the way you learn your lessons in life.

There are three components of being happy.

1. Do not allow any outward experience to influence you and how you feel about yourself. Do not engage with this negativity; just become an observer.

2. Live your life in the present, not in past experiences or future dreams and desires. You can do visualization practices, but remember to be like a kid. Don't think so much, just do it.

3. Make happiness your new habit. Say yes to life and experience all the different moments that life gives you.

A happy life is a chain of happy moments.

Make sure to set attainable goals; do not set goals that are so far and so high that they will cause you unhappiness due to their being unattainable. You don't want to feel like a failure.

It's also important to go for happiness, not relief. If you are chasing something just to receive instant gratification, which will not make you happy in the end. Instant gratification is just a way not to feel your negative emotions, but they will still be there.

When it comes to harmony, usually it includes other people. One important thing to remember is to not judge others, but instead, you need to accept them; they are playing their role in your life and on this earth.

In order to create harmony with another person, you must care enough about that person to hear her story, share her struggles, and be with her while the parts of her personality that are frightened come to the surface.

Your soul wants harmony with those you consider friends and those you consider enemies.

Harmony requires integrity; you cannot control others and make them become authentic, but you can decide whether or not you are Harmony with others is not always possible, but we should have the intention to attempt to create it with the people in our lives. Our intention is within our control; it does not depend on others. It is also important to remember that intention is not an expectation. We cannot expect to have harmony with everyone; harmony and expectation cannot coexist, but you can intend to be harmonious with people.

Integrity is also an important aspect of harmony. You must have the integrity to express yourself properly in order to create harmony. If you need to become angry in order to say no, or if you seek only to reject someone before you can be rejected, you cannot create harmony. Harmony requires the ability to say no and yes, perhaps with the intention of creating a caring, constructive, and joyful relationship.

Harmony requires courage. For example, if you care for someone, you will not allow them to speak to you disrespectfully. To create harmony does not require you to become a doormat for others; creating harmony requires the courage to fail the expectations of others, to object when you feel an objection is appropriate, and to say no, yes, or maybe without expectation.

The creation of harmony is spiritual activism; you devote your energy to what you believe, but you do not make others wrong, tolerate violence, or contribute to it, nor will you confuse kindness with weakness or your needs with love.

## RAISING YOUR FREQUENCY AND VIBRATION

Your emotions are created to reflect reality to you. Your emotions are one aspect of what creates your vibrations. Your vibrations can be negative or positive, depending on what you feel and what you're thinking.

Emotions are created by thought, and your emotions reflect your thoughts, and your thoughts are also a vibration. Some thoughts have a higher frequency, and some thoughts have a lower frequency. So, we need to find out what thoughts help us to feel good and what thoughts do not.

So if I walk into a situation and focus on what went wrong, for example, if someone is hurt in the hospital, then my frequency and vibration will be low, but if I focus on the positive or my good intentions or wishes, then my vibration is higher, and my vibration and frequency can support the situation.

If you are stuck in negative thoughts, go and meditate. Meditation will stop your thoughts or give you distance from them, then you will have more control and power to redirect your thinking. In meditation, it is important to just be a witness of whatever you are experiencing or thinking.

This state of being a witness is the key to gaining distance from your reactions in the moment and being able to choose how you want to redirect your vibrations. If meditation is too difficult because your mind is in a loop, then you can write down your feelings or do something called catharsis. Catharsis is when you give yourself a short amount of time to express irrational negative emotions; you can do this by screaming, punching, and crying. Afterward, you can meditate, and you will see that meditation is easier, especially if you are in total catharsis.

## SOME METHODS FOR CREATING HIGH VIBRATIONS AND FREQUENCIES:

1. Make conscious positive changes in your lifestyle, beliefs, fears, and judgments. And use your intuition in making these changes.

2. Listen to music that has a high frequency and makes you feel good.

3. Spend time with people or in places that have a high frequency. Examples of this can be spending time with wise men or women or being in nature around animals.

4. Do sports that make you feel good.

5. Participate in aroma or color therapy.

6. Write in a journal, making sure you keep it positive.

7. Constantly remind yourself to go to positivity and love.

8. Spend time in the water, the source of all creation. Walk by a beach, lake, or river.

9. Laugh and smile.

10. Accept life and the experiences it gives you.

# CHOICES

The center of the evolutionary process is choice. Choice is a quality and intention that you bring into everything that you think and do.

Your choice should be what you focus on. So, if you think and focus on the good things you will experience goodness. Your reality will furthermore manifest your desires.

Your personality has many different aspects. One aspect may be loving, patient, and generous while another may be jealous, annoying, and greedy. Each of these aspects have their own values and goals.

If you're not conscious about all your different sides, the unconscious sides or the sides you deny will grow and affect how you live your life and how you see reality.

As you become more honest and follow your feelings, you will become more aware of the different parts of yourself and the different things these parts want. You will see how these parts conflict inside of yourself, and, furthermore, how they affect what you end up receiving from existence, and how you perceive what you receive.

You cannot choose your choices consciously until you become conscious of all the different aspects of yourself. Once you have this awareness, your choices and intentions create a karmic path for you.

If you behave or speak in an angry way, you create more anger in your path, and if you are loving, you create more love in your path.

You are constantly getting support from the universe and your teachers to grow and become more conscious; it takes courage to choose to follow these signs and follow your heart.

Choice can also be defined as doing something that you are willing to take responsibility for.

Responsibility is making choices and being aware of how your choices will affect you and others. It's important to say to yourself, "I am responsible for the choices I make, and I am responsible for the consequences of these choices." This means asking yourself, "what will this produce?" and "what do I really want?" Then decide.

An unconscious choice is a reaction, an automatic response to a situation, and usually, it's driven by negative unconscious emotions. These reactions seem justified to you, no matter how they seem to others because they come from the unconscious parts of you.

A conscious choice is called a response, and a response is different than a reaction because it's made with intention. You are able to detach from the emotional charge of the situation. So, if you're able to respond, then you are able to make your unconscious feelings conscious, and you have more awareness and will learn something.

You can spend time doing all kinds of spiritual techniques, and they will help, but you cannot really grow until you start to take responsibility. In the end, responsibility and spirituality are the same because you must understand that you are responsible for what you create.

Make choices in life that bring more love into this world.

## INTUITION

Your insights, intuition, hunches, and inspiration are messages from the soul, or from advanced intelligence, that will assist your soul on its evolutionary journey.

We are here to experience and learn, so eventually, we can go back home to the universal love. Your intuition is the language of the soul. When you're in touch with your intuition, you're in touch with your soul, which is beyond time and space.

The first step in developing your intuition is to learn how to feel. You have to learn to calmly watch and feel what you are experiencing without reacting. Stop thinking or analyzing each situation; instead, feel the emotion of the event, begin to lesson to your heart and inside, the answer is your intuition. In the morning, as I sit still and ask my questions to the universe, the first answer that comes to me is what I need. To manifest my need is a matter of time, and it will be for the highest good for all (mine and others involved).

If you need guidance to do this, you can always ask for it. In meditation you can ask, "why do I feel this way?" and listen to the first answer that you can feel. This first answer is from your heart or soul. When you ask the universe for help, it always comes. Maybe you cannot understand the answer or maybe the answer will come in some unexpected way, but it will manifest itself.

The more you cleanse yourself emotionally, the more in touch you are with your intuition. Otherwise, unresolved feelings and negative thoughts can cloud your judgment. So, you can practice the emotion clearing exercises you've learned earlier in the book before going into meditation and asking yourself intuitive questions.

Your intuition helps you with survival instincts, hunches about danger, creativity, and inspiration. It is like a walkie-talkie that is connected to your soul.

## AUTHENTIC EMPOWERMENT

Human emotions are ultimately derived from two sources of basic feeling: Love and Fear. Positive emotions come from a space of love, and negative emotions come from a space of fear. Love is from your soul, and fear is from your ego. The needs of your soul are authentic, and the needs of your ego are, well, egoistic. The universe always meets your authentic needs, as the universe is constantly giving you opportunities to grow and be loved.

True power is not the ability to dominate another; it is an inner security.

The route to your true power is always though your emotions; only from your heart can you feel your true power. Furthermore, an empowered person is humble and kind.

The foundation of authentic power is forgiveness, clarity, humbleness, love, and wisdom.

Another aspect of power is the ability to forgive, the ability to let go of resentments, and baggage that you are carrying. It takes a lot to forgive those who have hurt you, but in doing it, you regain your own power because you do not hold them responsible for what you have experienced.

Clarity is happening when you're able to see your soul's purpose and other people with a sense of compassion and love.

Authentic, empowered people live in love. Love is the energy of the soul; love heals the personality. There is nothing that cannot be healed by love, and there is nothing but love.

The final piece of authentic power is finding your own higher wisdom.

In order to achieve this, you must learn to trust, relax about having to be in control, and know that the circumstances will come to you that are appropriate.

Remember, you can always ask your heart, the universe, God, etc., for guidance. You can always ask the wise souls that came before you for help.

There is so much love and wisdom around for us to learn from. We just need to ask for it.

Feel your intentions in your heart, not in your mind. Your heart is connected to divine intelligence and your mind is usually connected to your ego. Furthermore, when you feel fear, have the courage to look at what is underneath it. Don't stop at the fear because behind the fear is always the need for love. If you dig deeper into this fear, you will also be able to access your own love that wants to come out.

You can use your will to make choices that empower you rather than dis-empower you. You can also use your will to take responsibility for things, even when you feel angry or negative. This will allow you to choose to go in a different direction with your energy.

Powerlessness is the fear of not being lovable, not being worth it, or not finding a part in life. The pain stemming from this fear is very harmful, and until you become aware of this space inside of you and where it comes from and start to heal it, this space will always misshape your reality and your actions.

## MANIFEST YOUR DESIRES

There is a visionary process that allows you to manifest desires. Going through this process, allows you to program your subconscious to bring forth your reality. To achieve the best results from this process, you should do this five-minute process three times a day before mealtimes.

1. Sit in a meditation pose, close your eyes, and roll them towards your third eye. Then, start breathing slowly to bring your brain into an alpha state.

2. Think of a loving situation that happened in your life and allow yourself to feel it. Let a smile arise on your face and feel your heart.

3. Then visualize your desire, all aspects of it: the details, the feelings, the outcome—everything.

# CHAPTER 5

# Summary

When I was becoming New Me, I asked myself, "who am I, and where do I come from?"

I researched this question and thought about it. Well, shockingly, I learned that I am a little piece of the ultimate source, Tao. Tao is the ultimate energy source, or I prefer to call it God. Why do I say this? Because God, being the ultimate source and the creator of all, at one point decided to separate very tiny pieces of himself and say to these sparks, "Now you can be whatever you desire to be. You can go and experience all the good, bad, happy, and sad experiences that are possible and play all you want."

The purpose of being here is solely to experience intensity. Intensity is emotion; emotion is karma. By understanding karma and self-karma, you can go forward through the emotion of your life. Once you go through all these little experiences and different levels of evolutions to complete your journey, then you can go back to God as pure as he sent you.

As a spark, the spirit became a little soul and began a journey. The soul's first dimension is called the Etheric Dimension; the second dimension is called the Casual Dimension. The third dimension is the Mental Dimension, and the fourth is the Astral Dimension. Finally, the soul comes to the Physical Realm. I, the little soul as a mortal being with the help of my guides, started the journey of many lives, so my soul can learn the lessons from the experiences set forth. This little young soul separated from God into the universe and back again has seven main destinations. These are the universe's seven planes of creation. My little soul without any prior experience starts toward the school called "Earth" in a physical body, on a physical plane.

God created everything—every planet, every mineral, every plant, every animal, every human—and everything has a soul, so we know everything has a mortal soul and contains a part of God, and God only contains love; therefore, everything is love. Every soul is full of love, which is part of God.

Having said that about all souls, when we come across another creation of God, whether it is a mineral, plant, or human, all we should really see is their soul, which is love. The physical appearance is the uniform that they are wearing during this lifetime to experience what their soul wanted to learn.

The uniform that they appear to be wearing in this lifetime, the physical body that they appear to have, the personality that they are taking, the manner and behavior, are all the set of circumstances designed for that being in this lifetime. The experiences that they go through are all functions of their journey. Many times we get so involved in judging people and forget the fact that there should be no judgment. We forget to remember that what they are going through is their own soul journey. Yes, we can help and guide people to make better choices as they go through their journey, but we should also consider that they have their own experiences, and the best we can do is to enlighten them with our knowledge, help them to stay happy inside, and encourage them to make better choices.

The greatest universal power is consciousness, and the greatest thing we can do is to be working toward higher consciousness.

I noticed that my role is a KING, and I was born on October 13, so my zodiac sign is LIBRA. The characteristics of a king and Libra match my personality, and I have determined that my soul level is an old soul.

So, I am here at this time, in the school of Earth to experience certain tasks so my soul can be satisfied with the lessons set to be learned, and if I do not learn the lessons, the experiences will be repeated over and over in different shapes and forms until my soul gets satisfied. If you resist a lesson, it will take longer. What you fear the most will tend to happen to you until you no longer fear it, so be observant of all good and bad events in your life.

We should notice everyday things that happen and understand that we face different tasks and events. For a long time, we have been programmed to face these events logically and respond with our minds to these events. Sometimes we have a happy result, and sometimes we have an unpleasant result.

However, we should always respond to events with our soul, our intuition, and not our mind as this is what will allow us to grow in these situations.

Therefore, the next question we should logically ask after we learn to respond correctly to events is, "How do we know if these events are lessons from the soul's evolution or if they are from karmic events from past lives or this life?" You may not ever be able to figure out every situation. It is more important to realize that every situation is teaching you a lesson, and these lessons are meant to be learned from the soul's point of view and not your mind's point of view. From your mind's point of view, you analyze a task and come up with your best answer, but from the soul's point of view, you are learning through your emotion and feeling of the lesson of the events.

Have you ever noticed certain things happen to you that are similar, and you ask yourself "why?" You keep running into people with the same behavior, and you have the same interactions, or your jobs end up with the same results. The reason is that you're using your mind to solve or brush off the result, but your soul, which deals with feeling and emotion, was not used, so you did not receive the result of that lesson. You never stopped and truly learned the lesson; you dealt with the events intellectually and not from the soul's point of view. You did not thank the experience and bless it for helping you to learn the lesson. When those events came about, you left them with anger or disappointment, and, therefore, those lessons will get repeated until you feel them emotionally and your soul is satisfied and grateful for such lessons.

So, to simplify it, when things come up, take your time, relax, see how you feel about the situation, and feel the emotion of the others in this event. Then, with your universal intuition, respond to the emotion so that you not only satisfy your soul's need but also to the needs of others with a good intentional response, which creates a positive karma going forward. You may say that things go too fast in life, and there is not enough time to settle and listen to your soul view. However, there is always time. That is why there's a famous saying that 'wise men take their time'. They close their eyes, feel the emotion inside of them prior to responding too quickly. Sometimes they take a day or two to meditate and then respond.

New Me has an understanding that these events will take place and are part of life. Furthermore, we will experience less negative karma when we deviate less from our soul journey. The more grateful we are, the sooner we learn our lessons and avoid the repeats. By being kind, giving love, and sending blessings all at all times, we speak for our heart where our soul resides. If you can say or do everything from your heart, then you are improving your journey and all future journeys.

When things happen in our daily lives, we have the choice of how we respond to them. We can get angry, hateful, jealous, resentful, etc., but all of these negative reactions will bring us more of the same and will create more negative karma for ourselves. However, we can respond in a positive, loving, graceful way, which brings more positive energy and positive people and events. Make a conscious effort to have thoughts that will bring you good feelings and select your thoughts based on how they make you feel, rather than how popular or well-advertised they are. Only select the thoughts that make you feel best; your choice might be a beautiful sunset or mountain, or the face of someone you love. These thoughts that make you feel good replace the stressful moments and will bring you joy and love. It's important to make universal choices, which are good for all, and to have a good intention by doing so. What I mean by universal is that your thoughts and intentions are good not only for yourself but for anyone else involved. In fact, you should focus more on what benefits others, rather than yourself so others benefit. For example, if you are driving and someone pulls in front of you, and instead of apologizing, they flip a finger toward you, you have a choice to either react the same as they do or not. If you choose to react the same way, you now have created negative karma, which you will need to resolve some day.

But if you respond by blessing them and sending them love, you help them by creating a positive vibration, and their soul will benefit from your blessings. You just created positive karma, which will create the vibration for you to reap the benefits in the future.

The reason many beings reincarnate more often is that they make choices that create negative karma, and according to the law of circle, these karmas need to be resolved, so that our soul can move on to other experiences and evolve to a higher level of learning. Events take place because your soul needs to learn the experience, but you have the free will to choose how you will react and respond to these events.

Depending on the age of your soul, you will experience different things. If you are an infant soul, you will be experiencing survival, and you may be placed in a more remote area. You live many lives, reincarnating at the same age until you develop and move on to the baby soul level.

This continues until you go through all the levels of the soul.

Going back to what we talked about regarding lessons, it does not matter what we go through or how we go through them because we need to go through all of them to grow. You will never know the light until you experience the darkness. You will never know the rich until you experience the poor. You will never know the good until you experience the bad.

Imagine that going through life (meaning your soul going through all its destinations until you go back) is like you driving across the United States from NYC to LA. If you stay calm and happy and avoid getting lost, the distance is about 2,800 miles. Driving 10 hours a day on the main road, it will take you four days, but if you get lost or have problems along the way, it will not be fun and will take longer. This is what happens to our souls on their journey. It is important for the New Me to understand that life is about 2,800 miles with lots of challenges, accidents, roadblocks, and traffic jams, but for you to learn and move on, you must keep calm, bless people, and have fun going through it all.

When I began my journey as NEW ME, I asked myself two questions:

1.  What is my ROLE and my SOUL AGE?

2.  What can I do to live my life going forward with more balance, harmony, happiness, and good intentions aligned with the Universal Law?

The soul levels, as described earlier in the book, are stages that each soul will go through in order to reincarnate. Please note that there are experiences filled with good, bad, ugly, sad, and happy in each soul age. Remember, there are seven levels of soul age: Infant, Baby, Young, Mature, Old, Transcendental, and Infinite. Each soul age has seven levels or stages of progress and development, and each level or stage of development takes an average of three lifetimes, sometimes more than three lifetimes, depending on how the soul progresses through the lessons and experiences of each level. In total it takes about 200 lifetimes to go through all seven levels of soul ages.

Some souls choose to go through each stage of development much quicker and complete it in one lifetime in each stage; this may be attributed to them having less negative karmic payback and more positive deeds. New Me will help us to do the same, helping us choose wisely in order to advance our souls more quickly.

You may see that your role has the characteristics of a server and notice that you are always helping others, or you may always seek new things and determine your soul's role is that of an artisan. Understanding your role will help you to understand yourself better and become more of what you are.

This is the role you have chosen to take throughout your lifetimes. You do not change roles in any of your lives, so you will retain the same role characteristics. If you are a king, then you will remain king in all your reincarnations. If you are a warrior, you will stay the same.

It is very important to understand the big picture. By having the knowledge to begin to live more harmoniously, we can go through these levels in a shorter time because we will know better than to fight the lessons. We will appreciate what happened to us, responding with love and gratitude, giving love to others no matter what, and creating no bad karma for our future life.

## TO REMEMBER

NUMBER ONE: You are part of the universe as an individual soul experiencing emotional lessons on Earth school.

We originally separated from God in order for our soul to go through the process of incarnation on Earth. We were made to evolve spiritually, developing our talents. God gives us free will so that we would lovingly affirm our calling to be a co-creator with the Divine. We know that when we fulfill our reason, we will joyfully return to realms of the spirit to continue our soul's adventure.

Somewhere down this path, we fell from higher consciousness and pulled our attention away from the main path. Our ego began to act in a way opposite of our inner spirit, and while it did many good things, it also created some negativity. We harmed rather than helped, so by the law of the circle, we are not free to move on until we have paid off the karmic debts we now owe to others. Our soul needs to revisit those karmic encounters, lifetime after lifetime until we find a resolution.

So, our soul decides what lessons to learn and what karmas to resolve. It is very important throughout the whole process to be grateful because in gratitude you get aligned with your high consciousness and God.

Our soul, before it's born into this physical realm, makes decisions as to what its destiny will be and what lessons it will learn.

After our last physical death, before the new reincarnation, our souls get a chance to review their past lives with the help of "Guides." These spiritual guides, or guardian angels, review and analyze all of our prior experiences and karma. Your soul with the help of the guides decides what it can learn, determines what experiences need to occur for the soul to learn in the next physical realm, and chooses what would be best for the evolution of the soul.

> NUMBER TWO: Love yourself, parents, siblings, family members, neighbors, and every being that you come across God is all about love; the language of our soul is love; all there is in the higher dimension is love. Our souls want to be filled with as much love as possible to reincarnate and move on to the next stage. Therefore, the soul chooses where and how he or she can experience the lessons that it has chosen with the help of our guides prior to our reincarnation. This is so that we can experience and feel love to the greatest extent possible.

We choose our parents, our sex, our body style, our brothers and sisters, the family web, the relationship with all the members of our family, the place we are born, and the age we will die. We also choose our time of birth, which relates to astrological influences.

We may choose to return to those who have helped us grow in the past, maybe in order to learn forgiveness. We may return to someone who hurt us or did us wrong or another way around; we may return to someone we wronged, so we can make things right because relationships are so important and family relationships are so intense. It makes so much sense that the soul would want to return to the same relationships and make them right.

That is why returning to the same family and friends is a common thing throughout the reincarnation process. We connect to those we love and want to grow with them through our soul journey.

Through our relationships with our family, mates, bosses, coworkers, and partners, we have the greatest opportunity to resolve karma, especially the initial karma with our parents and siblings. We choose the parents and siblings that we need to best resolve our karma and to provide us the best opportunity to experience the lessons that our soul desires. This time around we may be the parents that we had during our last life, or we may interchange positions with siblings, friends, or family members. We also have a chance to meet many new individuals for our soul evolution and growth. Remember, we need to love anyone that is placed in our lives, whether our souls knew them in a past life or not.

One thing is for certain in all incarnation studies, you are totally responsible for who and what you are in this lifetime.

The best and most effective approach to all is Love, so if you realize why everyone is around you and understand that there is a reason they are there, then you can start to identify the past karmas needed to be resolved.

Ask yourself why you chose these parents, keep going deeper, and find the reasons and the lessons you learned during this process. Was it kindness? Was it forgiveness? Was it love? Was it to make up for any wrongdoing, either yours or theirs? Was it how close you were together or how far you have come over time? No matter what, it is important for your evolution and happiness. You love your parents, so be grateful and thankful to them for being part of your life. They helped your growth and provided the circumstances, so your soul can learn the lessons needed.

You chose your siblings and your relationship with them. This again was so you could learn what you needed for your soul to progress. Your soul wanted to learn from this relationship, and theirs wanted to learn as well.

Cherish this relationship and remember it is best to resolve all past karma by feeling the emotion you are supposed to. No matter what, you should give love at all times, as well as forgiveness and gratitude, so you can clear the past and create good karma for the future.

The same thing can be said about your relationship with your friends, teachers, coworkers, bosses, neighbors, and everyone you come across in life. They are all part of your life and play a role in your learning lessons.

Be grateful, thankful that no matter what you should give love to all.

Please note that everything that happens around you is designed for you to pay your karmic debt for your soul evolution, so no matter who you come close to, bless them no matter what, send love, send light, and be grateful for all that has taken place. In this way you can know that you will learn the lesson you are supposed to learn.

Love yourself, and all things you desire are possible.

> **NUMBER THREE:** Know yourself, know how to respond, and know your intention.

1. What should I know?

I should know that I am part of God with all the knowledge and ability to do as I desire, but because of my past life karma and my soul's desire to learn the lessons it needs, I am in this lifetime. What I do or think has consequences. If I do good things and if I live my life according to universal life, my future will consist of all good deeds.

2. How should I respond?

My reaction to these events is in my control; things happen every day, good, bad, or ugly events, and my response is in my control. I should not react instinctively and quickly because my reactions are most likely from my mind, and I need to respond with my emotions from my soul and heart. From my soul's point of view, I should see how I feel, feel the emotion that is created inside of me because of this event, listen to my intuition and heart, and respond to this event from my intuitive source.

The New Me responds from the heart with love. By emitting good, positive vibrations, we will attract the same and satisfy our soul's needs. We must experience all situations peacefully and stay calm and happy inside.

3. What should my intention be?

When we come across an event, first we should observe and digest this event, situation, or person fully, to the best of our ability, rather than rushing to conclusions or reacting quickly. Taking our time, we need to ask our soul what it is that we may learn from this. Then, we should listen to the inner voice and our heart, feel the energy and the emotion, consider ONLY the Universal Law (Dharma) as our guide, use the inner voice of our soul and respond accordingly to every situation. You will find that your fairness, love, kindness, and gratefulness will resolve these situations, and inner peace has more satisfaction than any victory. Your intention should always be with love.

## DAILY NOTES FOR NEW ME

1. As you wake up early:

- Do your breathing meditation (preferably barefoot and outdoors).

- Do your first three chakra alignments in order to begin to have a good flow of energy from your heart chakra to your higher chakra and intentional source.

- Connect to an intentional source (your higher self and the ultimate source of knowledge). Sit quietly; ask the universe the source to guide and help you with your questions, problems, and goals to bring you what is good for your highest good. You are not alone, nor do you have all the answers, but by connecting to your higher self, the intentional source, you are tapping to all possibilities and asking God to solve your tasks and guide you.

As you mention your problem the first answer is your guide, have faith, and follow-through.

2. During your daily life:

- Bless and love whatever you come across. No judgment, accept all things as is.

- Slow down, digest, and feel the emotion of any events crossing you. Do not react from your mind; react from your heart, and if you can respond, do so. Otherwise, postpone responding to the events to another time until you can feel the emotion and respond from the soul point of view.

- Be calm. The best medicine for anxiety, stress, and depression is silence and meditation; observe throughout the day and pray for all beings.

- Make a conscious choice to select good thoughts that bring you good feelings, no matter how stressful events are. Replace your thought selection with good thoughts that brings you good feelings to make good choices.

- Make all your decisions based on the Universal Law. Do more for others than you receive. In every dealing, think of what good you can do for others. Seek to benefit them more than yourself. When you have to make a choice to be Kind or Right, push the ego's demand back and select to be Kind.

3. Before going to sleep:

- Rewind and reflect on all the things that happened during the day and all the people you met. Feel the energy and emotion. Bless the people you met and send love to all.

- Before going to sleep ask for forgiveness from all people you have ever done wrong to and send the light and love out into the universe.

- My mom and dad have passed away, and I ask their soul to help and guide me with my problem. You can do the same if you have lost people who were close to you.

### ALWAYS REMEMBER:

The more you send love, the more you receive love.

The more you bless, the more you get blessed.

The more you give gratitude, the more you receive gratitude.

The more you forgive, the more you get forgiveness.

This New Me will see immediate inner peace results, and before you know it, you will have a new way of being. Going forward you will see things without judgment and feel things with your heart.

In this book, I tried to explain many important subjects: love, fear, happiness, desire, harmony, anger, etc. At any time that you feel the need, please go back and read about that particular subject or feel free to research it on your own.

Remember, in life, there are only two things that make us decide what to do: love and fear.

Love is the language of your soul, and fear comes from a lack of knowledge or the unknown. When we know things or have an understanding of things, then there is no fear. Our purpose as a New Me is to have better knowledge, less fear, and choices that are made with love.

I urge you to have faith and trust in God; ask for help, ask for guidance, and ask for direction. There are resources there to help, all you need to do is ask. Do not try to solve all of your problems with the same mind that got you into these problems. With God there, you can have no fear or anxiety about anything.

Thank you for allowing me to share my love, gratitude, and wisdom.

My true intention in New Me is to bring you, and the world, a better understanding of who we are and love, joy, and happiness for your entire soul cycle.

With Love,
David Niroo

# Acknowledgments

I would like to acknowledge Pasha Niroo, my youngest son who is on a high spiritual journey, helping and teaching people to be happy inside and to deal with all events of life with love. Pasha has helped me in editing this book from beginning to end. I couldn't do it without him. I am deeply grateful for his loving presence in my life.

For my publisher, Atlantic Publishing Group, that believed in this book from the beginning and did their best to make it all happen.

I also want to thank Michael for his teachings and Paramahansa Yoganada for Self-Realization Fellowship.

To my wife, Haleh, who has been there for almost 30 years, supporting me in every aspect of my path and inspiring me with love to write this book.

# About the Author

David Niroo was born on October 13, 1950, in Tehran, Iran. He came to the United States to receive a higher education and follow his American dream. Through hard work and compassion, David accomplished great financial success. David is a natural-born motivator and leader who seeks the path of understanding to answer his life's questions and strives to have knowledge of the spiritual world. These endeavors have given him peace, joy, and harmony in his life. In New Me, he shares his findings.